P9-BZE-782

A Fireside Book

Learn to Read Music

By HOWARD SHANET

Associate Professor of Music, Columbia University, and Conductor of the University Orchestra

A Fireside Book
Published by Simon and Schuster

Grateful acknowledgment is made of the help of Henry W. Simon, who has gone over this book with the painstaking attention to detail not only of a publisher but of a musician and a writer, and with such remarkable tact that in the process he has become a friend.

TWELFTH PAPERBACK PRINTING

SBN 671-21027-0 FIRESIDE PAPERBACK EDITION
LIBRARY OF CONGRESS CATALOG CARD NUMBER: 55-11046
MANUFACTURED IN THE UNITED STATES OF AMERICA

CONTENTS

PREFACE

Many people who love music and have a wide hearing acquaintance with it suffer from a feeling of inferiority because they cannot read music and are timid about asserting their opinions in the company of musicians. They may have excellent taste and judgment concerning what they hear, but they wilt before the professional because of his technical knowledge. The layman in literature and art will stand up for his ideas, but the poor music lover is apt to back down and feel that somehow he has got beyond his depth. So music becomes something mysterious to him and the musician a strange fellow who lives in a world different from his.

Obviously, musicians are the best judges of music, but non-professional opinion should not be brushed aside. The layman is the consumer and patron and what he thinks is important. He will find that with technical knowledge music loses none of its magic, but he will be able to see through some of the hocus-pocus now. The ability to read music is the first step and can make him feel that what he has to say about programs and performances is entitled to the professional's respect.

Educators think wistfully that some day notation may be taught in the elementary schools along with the alphabet. Children could master it easily, and many of them would have a lifetime of pleasure from the skill. But it is not being done, and the concert halls are filled with eager people who have found out too late that they are missing something important.

To these frustrated individuals, Howard Shanet's Learn to Read Music *will come as a happy surprise. Not only because of its clarity and competence but also because of the author's infectious spirit of optimism, the reader will arrive at confidence and hope.*

DOUGLAS MOORE,
MacDowell Professor of Music
Columbia University

WHAT THIS BOOK WILL DO

THIS LITTLE BOOK is intended to teach adults the fundamentals of reading musical notation.

If you follow its instructions seriously and carefully, you should learn all the important symbols used in printed music and how they are put together to represent tunes. By the time you have finished, you should be able to pick up a song book or a piece of sheet music and find the tunes at the piano.

Don't expect more at first, but don't expect less either.

These lessons *won't* teach you to sing beautifully, or to play the piano or the bazooka. But if printed music has been a mystery to you, a mystery you've always wanted to understand, some strange hieroglyphics you've seen on Christmas cards and advertisements (usually written wrong, by the way!), then the study of these pages will enable you to take any simple melody in musical notation and work out the meanings of the symbols for yourself.

I promise.

HOW THIS BOOK CAME
TO BE WRITTEN

IN MANY YEARS as a conductor and teacher, I had become convinced that thousands of people everywhere regarded music reading as a dark secret at which they looked longingly and hopelessly from afar. What a shame, I often thought, because it's really such an easy thing to learn. So when I had to teach music-appreciation classes for students with no previous musical training at Hunter College in New York, I experimented by adding to the required work a condensed course in music reading. *I found that I could give serious adults this information in four one-hour classes!* This was not just an idle theory or a dream. In my years at Hunter, I taught hundreds of students every semester according to this system.

But it was in Huntington, West Virginia, when I was conductor of the symphony orchestra there, that I finally tested my methods on the general public. On Sunday, February 3, 1952, the people of Huntington were startled to read in giant letters, spread across all eight columns of their newspapers, the following headline:

LEARN TO READ MUSIC IN ONE EASY LESSON—
FREE

The papers went on to explain that it really would be one *hard* lesson, but that the offer was made in good faith.

Huntington is the hub of a tri-state area and the news

spread quickly to towns in West Virginia, Ohio, and Kentucky, within a radius of a hundred miles. Here is how one newspaper described the events which followed:

> People turned out in such numbers that the little Marshall College Science Hall, reserved for the occasion, could not accommodate the knowledge-seekers, and the course had to be moved to the East High School Auditorium where 1000 eager adults formed a giant "class" of serious and attentive students.
>
> In one marathon lesson, which lasted from 7 to almost 11 P.M., teacher Shanet gave his 1000 pupils all the elements of reading simple printed music, so that by the end of the session people who had known absolutely nothing at all about music were able to go to the piano keyboard and pick out—slowly but surely—the tunes of hymns, patriotic airs, and popular sheet-music favorites. Demonstration pieces ranged from "Old Hundred" and "America" to hit-parade numbers like "Shrimp Boats" and "Cry." The only materials required for the students were pencil and paper for taking notes.

Interestingly enough, it was the professional musicians, aware that music is a lifetime study, who were skeptical before I began. But it really wasn't a gamble; after all, I had tried the same methods many times in my Hunter College days.

As the news of our experiment spread, a deluge of mail poured in from every part of the country. At the height of the excitement 150 letters a day were coming in! Music educators, publishers, and just plain people wanted to know what methods had been used, how they could try them for themselves, and whether the system could be put into book form.

For a long time I hesitated to attempt this sort of instruction in writing. I was afraid that, without the live presence of the teacher and without the possibility of playing or singing examples for the student, it would be a clumsy business to convey this information with the printed page alone.

But the tremendous need and demand for such instruction finally changed my mind. I believe with my teacher, the late Dr. Serge Koussevitzky, that music is for everyone. Music reading is a fundamental skill which should be taught to all children in elementary schools, just as arithmetic is taught to all. If it is not—and apparently thousands of adults in every city have missed it—then we have to do something about it.

When you have gone through this study the hard way, lifting yourself by your own mental bootstraps, perhaps you will fight to have this sort of instruction put into the public schools in your community.

Good luck, colleague.

HOW TO USE THIS BOOK

1. Have pencil and paper handy and write down each new point you learn. Later you will need some lined music paper, so a supply of it has been bound right into the last pages of this book for your convenience; but at first, ordinary unlined paper will be sufficient. You will find that writing down the material not only will help you to remember it, but will also automatically make an outline of the course if you save your notes and jottings. *Write down everything, even if you seem to find it easy at the first glance;* often even the easy things have a way of vanishing an hour or so later, unless you reinforce the first impressions by the device of writing them down.

2. You must concentrate and work seriously. Just sitting there with a book in front of you won't be enough. It's really simple stuff, but *you* have to do it; no one else can do it for you.

3. In addition to the pencil and paper, you will need just two props: (a) about ten feet of strong twine or string (for Part II), (b) occasional use of a piano (chiefly for Parts II and III). If you don't have one at home, look around now for the nearest friend or relative who does, and reserve a few hours of time at his instrument.

PART ONE

Notation of Rhythm

1   Fortunately, the system of musical notation divides into two clear parts: a way of indicating **rhythm** (how long the different tones last) and a way of indicating **pitch** (how high or low the different tones are).

I say "fortunately" because this permits us to study each part separately, so that we can deal with simple things at the start.

We shall begin with the notation of rhythms because the system used is so straightforward and easy to learn that anyone can pick it up in a few hours.

FIRST STEPS

2   With the toe of your foot, tap steadily four beats or pulses, at about the speed of a military march, over and over again, like this:

ONE-two-three-four, ONE-two-three-four, ONE-two-three-four,

❙ ❘ ❘ ❘ ❙ ❘ ❘ ❘ ❙ ❘ ❘ ❘

Make the **ONE** heavier than the other three beats each time— *not slower,* mind you, because they must be equal in time and speed, just heavier or more forceful so that you feel where each group of four begins.

3   Now while you keep up the steady tapping, sing one long tone, holding it as long as you can without straining. Just sing *Da* or *Ta,* the way people do when they are singing a tune without words. Suppose we agree on *Ta* for the moment. It doesn't even matter whether you sing a high sound or a low one, since we are concerned only with the lengths of tones right now; so just sing the first sound that comes into your head, any one that is comfortable for you, use the syllable *Ta* to sing it on, instead of words, and make it one long sound:

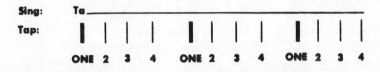

Sing: **Ta** _____

Tap:

ONE 2 3 4 **ONE** 2 3 4 **ONE** 2 3 4

4   Next, let's try tones of differing lengths. For the following exercise, begin tapping in the same way as before, but this time hold each tone only as long as the line after it indicates. In other words, each *Ta* will be held while four beats go by, and there will be four such *Ta*s altogether:

Sing: Ta _____ **Ta** _____ **Ta** _____ **Ta** _____

Tap:

Remember that the tapped beats must go by in a steady march, all at the same speed; and each *Ta* syllable is sung to four of these beats or taps.

5   When this seems comfortable and natural to you, go on to the next exercise, which involves even shorter tones, each syllable being held for only two beats:

Sing: Ta _ **Ta** _ **Ta** _ **Ta** _ **Ta** _ **Ta** _ **Ta** _ **Ta** _

Tap:

6   After this, try combining the two types, as follows:

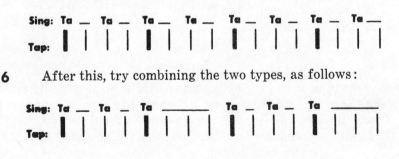

Sing: Ta _ **Ta** _ **Ta** _____ **Ta** _ **Ta** _ **Ta** _____

Tap:

7   Now add a third kind, in which each tone is held for the length of one single beat or tap. We can combine it immediately with one of the longer types, just for the sake of variety:

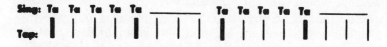

8   In fact, while we are at it, we can work out all sorts of combinations of these patterns. Make some up for yourself, and also try to read the following examples. Do each one a few times, until it is easy and almost automatic for you:

These three, by the way, are actually taken from the rhythms of well-known tunes. Number 1 is the beginning of the famous round, "Frère Jacques." Number 2 is the beginning of the hymn, "Holy, Holy, Holy, Lord God Almighty." And number 3 is part of the "Jingle Bells" chorus, slowed down a bit.

9   In each of these cases, two rhythms are going on simultaneously: the steady tapping of the beats, and the freer pattern of each tune's rhythm which you sing above the tapping. The underlying rhythm represented by the steady tapping is called the **meter,** from the Latin word meaning "to measure," because it supplies a unit of measurement against which the more irregular rhythm of the tune itself can be judged or observed. Each recurring group of beats is called a **measure;** for example, one group of four beats or pulses, such as you tapped out with your foot, represents a measure.

10   Sometimes, instead of the word *measure,* you will find the word *bar* used. This arises from the fact that measures are separated from each other, in musical notation, by vertical lines or bars, like this:

Originally the word *bar* referred only to the line itself, but by a kind of substitution it has come to be used occasionally as though it meant the same thing as *measure.* Even professional musicians do this so frequently that it now has become accepted usage. Thus, you may hear musicians speaking of music which has "four beats in a bar," or "four beats in a measure."

A **double bar,**   ‖ ,

is used to mark the end of a composition or of an important part of it.

11   Now for the actual symbols used in the notation of musical rhythms:

NOTE SYMBOLS

The basic symbol is the one used to represent the time consumed in four beats (such as you tapped out in each exercise), and it is called a **whole-note.** It looks like a horizontal oval in print, ◯ , although when written by hand it is usually made with two strokes, one for the upper half and one for the lower half, ◯. (You will find when you try it that this makes it a little easier to place the note neatly on the lines used in music.) A whole-note is used whenever one wishes to represent a single continuous sound which lasts four beats. Try it this way. Tap four beats with your foot, and at the same time sing one long sound — just sing *Ta*, as we did for the previous exercises — while you tap four beats:

When a musician sees this oval note in a piece of music, he knows immediately that he must sound one long tone which uses up four beats.

12   To represent a shorter sound, one which lasts only half that long, a modification of the oval symbol is made by adding a *stem* to it: ♩

Whenever you see this symbol, a sound lasting two beats is required. Try it in the same way. Sing *Ta*, but stop after you have tapped just twice.

You now have sung a **half-note.** Two of them together obviously will take as long as one whole-note, as simple arithmetic will tell you:

Try it by singing *Ta* over two beats, and then immediately going on to another *Ta* for two more beats:

It is exactly the same pattern that you were singing in Section 5 (page 2).

13   If we want to represent a sound that is still shorter — a **quarter-note** (one half the value of a half-note) — a further modification of the symbol is needed. For this purpose, the stem of the note is retained but the "head" is filled in, instead of being left hollow:

♩ quarter-note

This sound lasts only one beat. If you sing *Ta* each time you tap, you will have sung four quarter-notes as you tap **ONE**-two-three-four:

Two of these short notes add up to the same amount of time as a half-note, and four of them equal a whole-note. In other words, ♩ ♩ ♩ ♩ consumes as much time as ♩ ♩ ,

or o .

14   All the exercises we did in Sections 4, 5, 6, 7, and 8 can
be written in rhythmic notation with the aid of the symbols
we have just learned. Notice the bar lines separating measures from each other, and the double bar which marks the
end of a piece of music or of an important subdivision:

"Frè-re Jac-ques"   *(Same as Sec. 8, No. 1)*

"Ho-ly Ho-ly   Ho -   ly"

(Same as Sec. 8, No. 2)

"Jin-gle Bells"

(Same as Sec. 8, No. 3)

15   Proceeding further, we next take half of a quarter-note, i.e., an **eighth-note,** the symbol for which is formed by adding a "hook" to the stem of the quarter-note:

Of course, two of these equal one quarter-note, four of them equal one half-note, and eight of them equal one whole-note.

When we sound eighth-notes, there will be *two* sounds for each tap or beat, since two of them go by in the time of one quarter-note. In other words, as you tap each beat, you will have to sing quickly *Ta-ta:*

Ta - ta   Ta - ta   Ta - ta   Ta · ta

Sing:

Tap:

16   After this point in the system, the further subdivisions are even simpler and more logical. A **sixteenth-note** is formed from the eighth-note symbol by merely adding another hook to the stem: ♪ . Now we are getting into fairly rapid sounds, for we must get four of these notes into the space of a single beat:

Ta- ta- ta- ta Ta- ta- ta- ta   Ta- ta- ta- ta   Ta- ta- ta- ta

Sing:

Tap:

Be sure to keep the beats at the same speed as before, or the whole point will be missed. You tap exactly as in the previous cases, **ONE**-two-three-four, but you sing four rapid *Ta*s to each beat. Two sixteenth-notes fill the same amount of time as one eighth-note; four sixteenths the same time as one quarter-note; eight sixteenths as one half-note; sixteen sixteenths as one whole-note.

17   Next in value is the **thirty-second-note**, which is half as
long as a sixteenth, and is written with three hooks :

Arithmetic reminds us that there are four thirty-seconds to
every eighth-note, eight of them to every quarter-note, sixteen of them to a half-note, thirty-two of them in a whole-
note.

18   We can go on to **sixty-fourth-notes** by adding another hook

and after that to **128th-notes** and even further by the same
process, but there isn't much practical point to it, because in
the first place, the notes get so rapid after the sixty-fourth-
note stage that not many singers or players can produce
them (try it yourself!), and in the second place, there comes
a point after which the listener even has difficulty in dis-
tinguishing them. That is, they give the illusion, if they are
too fast, of all running together into one long trembling
sound. It is a somewhat similar phenomenon in *hearing* to
what happens in *sight* when a series of still photographs is
run so rapidly that the separate images seem to blend into
one moving picture.

19   Let's stop at this point, for just a moment, to summarize
in table form the set of note values we have learned so far:

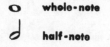

o   **whole-note**

d   **half-note**

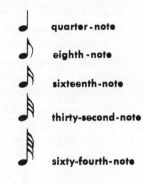

♩   quarter-note

♪   eighth-note

♬   sixteenth-note

   thirty-second-note

   sixty-fourth-note

COMBINATIONS OF NOTE SYMBOLS

20   These symbols can be combined in various ways to form rhythmic patterns. We already have seen how the whole-note, half-note, and quarter-note may be combined (page 7). Here are three examples which add eighths and sixteenths in combination with the others. *If these, and the examples on the next several pages seem difficult to read right now, don't worry about it. They are given at this point chiefly by way of illustration; a little later, we will actually practice reading such combinations, but for the moment it is not expected that you will get all the details right, and it is not intended that you spend a great deal of time on them — just enough to give you an idea of the relatively longer sound of certain kinds of notes as compared with others.*

1.

In the first measure, each *Ta* that we sing (quarter-note) corresponds with one tapped beat. In the second measure, however, we have eighth-notes, which means that we must sing *Ta-ta* — two notes — each time that we tap a beat at the original speed. Try just those two measures first. As you tap steadily, **ONE**-two-three-four, **ONE**-two-three-four, sing with the first group of four beats *Ta Ta Ta Ta,* one to each beat, as indicated by the notation. But when you come to the second group of four beats, sing *Ta-ta* in the time that it takes for each beat to go by. Be sure that you keep the underlying taps in the second measure exactly the same as the four in the first measure.

Now take the last two measures. Measure 3 is the same as measure 1 — four simple quarter-notes, one to each beat, and measure 4 is a pattern we have already done on page 7 — half-notes held for two beats each. Read the whole exercise. Keep the beats going steadily, as though you were keeping time for a march. And don't pause between measures; just fit the sung syllables over the beats as you tap them.

21   Another exercise, with slightly different combinations:

The first measure has only one difference from the first measure of the preceding exercise — its second beat is divided into two eighth-notes. Therefore, we will sing one *Ta* to each beat, except for the second beat where we will sing *Ta-ta* in the time of one beat. Try that measure alone a few times. The second measure begins with eighth-notes. On each of its first two beats, you must sing the two eighth-notes, *Ta-ta*. Then, over the next two beats of the measure, you hold one long half-note. Do this measure by itself a few times, keeping the beats tapping regularly, and singing over them the four fast eighth-notes followed by the held half-note:

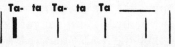

The third measure is still different: it is almost like the measure of eighth-notes which we read in the preceding exercise, except that here the first beat is not subdivided but remains a quarter-note. You must sing just one *Ta* on the first beat of the measure, therefore, but a *Ta-ta* on each other beat. The last measure is the familiar pattern of two half-notes, which also ended the other exercise. Now read the whole line, keeping the beats strictly in time as you tap them, and fitting the various note-values to them as they go by.

22 Here, finally, is one with sixteenth-notes:

3.

The first measure is the simple relationship of four equal quarter-notes, one to each beat. Measure 2, you may notice, is exactly the same as the second measure in the exercise we just finished, so all you must do is repeat the pattern already learned of four eighths followed by a half-note. Measure 3 begins like measure 2, with its first two beats divided into eighth-notes, but each of its last two beats is divided even further into sixteenth-notes. Therefore, you must sing *Ta-ta* to each of the first two beats, but *Ta-ta-ta-ta* − notes twice as rapid! − on each of the other two beats. You probably will find that the four sixteenth-notes must be sung just about as rapidly as your tongue will permit, if you are to get them into one beat. Singing them very lightly will help.

The last measure consists of one long whole-note over all four of the beats. Read the whole line now, taking care not to alter the steady pulse of the tapped beats even when the top line grows difficult.

ADDITIONAL SYMBOLS

23   Let's continue with the symbols. The system still has some gaps. For instance, you will notice that each value is half or double one of the others. But suppose we want to represent a sound that is the length of *three* quarter-notes. We have no single symbol for a sound of this duration, and it will not be sufficient to place two of our symbols side by side, like this,

as you might assume at first glance, because they represent two separate sounds, not one continuous tone:

To get around this problem, and to avoid inventing a new symbol for each value not covered by the old ones, one new general symbol is introduced which indicates that two of the old ones are being combined or added together to form a longer value. It is called a **tie**, and looks like this: ⌣ or ⌢. When two symbols are tied together, the reader understands that he is to sing one single sound of a length equal to the sum of the tied notes. For example,

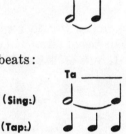

lasts for three beats:

(Sing:)
(Tap:)

The same result could be produced by writing

although it is not quite so economical since it requires the writing of one extra note and one extra tie. The effect of the tie is to convert two or more old symbols into one composite symbol, with a value equal to their sum:

In measure 1 and in measure 3, the tie produces one long sound lasting three beats.

In the following example, the tie produces a long tone which straddles the bar line:

24   This principle of tying notes together gives us a great many new values, because notes of all sorts may be combined to produce new lengths. Here is an example of a whole-note tied to a half-note:

The long tone at the beginning lasts for a measure and a half.

Following are a few other examples of tied notes, in addition to ♩ ♩ and ○ ♩

Later we will work with many such tied notes as they occur in our exercises.

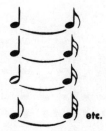

etc.

25 However, another area still remains uncovered by symbols. We can now add together existing ones to create notes of "uneven" values, but we have no way of *dividing* notes except by halves. For example, we can divide a quarter-note into halves (i.e., into eighth-notes), but how could we divide a quarter-note into thirds? Or into fifths? How could we indicate the division of a half-note or a whole-note into thirds or fifths or sevenths of its original length, instead of into halves as we have done until now?

Again, in order to avoid the creation of a whole new set of symbols for these values, one new device is added which will work for all divisions of a note-value into an odd number of parts. The method can best be explained by an illustration. Let's assume that we want to divide a quarter-note into three parts instead of two. We simply take the symbol for dividing it in half (the eighth-note), write *three* of them, and label them with a number *3* over or under a bracket, like this:

(called a **triplet**).

This is understood, by convention, to say: "These may look like eighth-notes, but they really aren't. They are thirds of a quarter-note as is confirmed by the number under them, and we have borrowed the eighth-note symbol only because it is the next smaller symbol available below a quarter-note." The trick in reading these triplets is to sing three equal notes, *Ta-ta-ta* in the time of one beat. Simply tap the four steady beats, as usual, and fill one of them with the *Ta-ta-ta* where indicated:

26   The method can be generalized as follows: *To divide any given note-value into an odd number of equal parts, (a) take the symbol for the next smaller value, (b) write as many of those symbols as are indicated by the odd number, and (c) label the resulting group of symbols with that odd number over a bracket which covers the group.* For example: To divide a half-note into fifths, take the next smaller value below the half-note (i.e., the quarter-note), write five such quarter-notes, cover them with a bracket, and write the number *5* over the bracket as a final reminder that they aren't to be read as real quarter-notes (half of a half-note) but as fifths of a half-note:

♩ ♩ ♩ ♩ ♩ (called a **quintolet** or **quintuplet**).

Instead of a bracket, some musicians used to use an ordinary tie, like the one described on page 15. This practice frequently led to confusion, since the tie instructs the reader to bind symbols together, and the purpose of the new device is almost the opposite — to indicate a group of notes formed by *division* of a given note, not combination. Therefore, most careful musicians have abandoned the use of the tie for this meaning, and have substituted the bracket; but the student should keep on the lookout, especially in older music, for cases in which the tie is used in this ambiguous way.

27   We have now covered almost all the important symbols used for the time values of sounds, but there are two shorthand devices which must be explained here for convenience and completeness.

a). The **dot.** In music, as in language, certain combinations of elements are found to be more frequent than others. In most European languages, for example, the letter *e* occurs more frequently than any other, *q* generally is followed by *u*, etc. Similarly, in music, the rhythmic combination of a note tied to half its own value is very common; e.g., a half-note tied to a quarter, or a quarter tied to an eighth :

Since the writing of music is a slow and tedious process (just think how many marks the composer must put on paper to represent the sounds made at a single instant by the hundred players of a symphony orchestra), musicians constantly strive for shorthand methods of indicating standard combinations. In writing the combinations shown above, they often shorten the symbols by substituting just a dot, in each case, for everything after the first note. Thus:

Both the tie and the entire second note are dropped in each instance, and it is understood that the dot takes their place. Not only does this save the strokes required to write the tie and the stem (and a hook, too, in the second case), but the tiny dot is quicker and easier to make than the head of the real note it replaces. This may not seem like a tremendous difference at first, but the saving of time and work is really appreciated when one has to write a great many such combinations.

In short, then, the dot is really a quick way of indicating that the first note is to be lengthened by tying to it a note of half its own value. For a dotted half-note, therefore, add a quarter to the original half. For a dotted quarter, add an eighth to the quarter. For a dotted eighth, add a sixteenth to the eighth, etc. The example on page 15, for instance, instead of being written:

$$♩\smallsmile♩\ ♩\ ♩|♩\ ♩|♩\ ♩\smallsmile♩\ ♩\ ♩|o\ \|\ .$$

could also be written:

$$♩.\qquad ♩|♩\ ♩\ |♩.\qquad ♩|o\ \|$$

Similarly, $♩\ ♪$

means the same thing as $♩.$

and $♪\ ♪$

means the same thing as $♪.$

Observe that the dot can *not* be used to add some less usual fraction to a given note. There is no short way of indicating $♩\ ♪$,

for example, since the sixteenth is not half of the half-note, and really no short way is needed since this combination doesn't happen often enough to warrant a shorthand symbol.

28   Occasionally you may come across a *double-dotted* note, like this: $♩..$

The same rule applies here. That is, the first dot adds half the original note (or an additional quarter-note), *and the second dot adds half the first dot* (another eighth-note), making a total of

Similarly

equals

29   b). The **beam.** When several notes in a group require hooks on their stems (eighths, sixteenths, thirty-seconds, etc.), musicians often try to reduce the numerous separate strokes which these hooks make necessary in writing. This is done by making one big set of hooks, called *beams,* to be shared by all the stems, as follows:

Instead of ___ we often have ___

Instead of ___ we often have ___

Instead of ___ we often have ___

Instead of ___ we often have ___

The notations in the left-hand column are still possible, but those on the right are easier, more readily legible, and therefore more frequent. For instance, the example on page 13, instead of being written:

would more often be written:

RESTS

30   We now have a complete system for representing the duration of sounds, but in music the silences are of equal importance. Imagine what catastrophes would occur in an
orchestra if the trumpet player, for instance, played the
notes of his part correctly but did not wait the proper number
of beats of silence, so that he came blaring in before the
flute or the violin had finished.

The symbols for indicating the duration of silences are
called **rests** and there is a whole set of them to correspond
with the note symbols listed in our table above. Here is the
table of rests placed side by side with the notes for the sake
of comparison:

The whole-rest is just a horizontal bar suspended below one
of the lines on which music is written. The half-rest is the
same kind of bar, but sitting on top of the line instead of
suspended below it. The quarter-rest is so different from any
other symbol in music (or out of it!) that it can't be mis-
taken for anything else; it looks a bit like the letter *Z* back-
wards, as you will notice. The eighth-rest is very much like

an eighth-note without the head, as though to say: "Here is an eighth-note but with no real sound." The remainder of the hooked rests, as the table shows, simply add hooks to the basic pattern established by the eighth-rest.

31   Ties are not necessary for rests, as a moment of reflection will make clear, because one silence will flow smoothly into another without the need of a tie! — one has simply to write the desired number of rests one after the other. For similar reasons the beam is not used with rests (the successive short ones would simply add up to one longer rest, anyway), but the dot can be used to indicate a rest which is half again as long as one of the given symbols: e.g.,   ↓· for ↓ ↱

꘏· for ꘏ Ꙩ

↱· for ↱ ꘏

32   For very long rests of many measures, there are two methods in use: the simplest is to draw a long horizontal line with a vertical stop at each end, and to mark over it the number of whole measures of rest.

┠──13──┨

A fussier way is to use a thick vertical bar (filling the space between two of the lines used in writing music) to represent each two measures of silence:

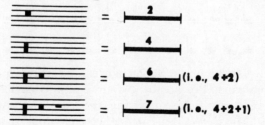

COMBINATIONS OF NOTES AND RESTS

33   Do the following exercises, which show how notes and rests are used together:

Here the first measure consists of one whole-note held for the full four beats of the measure. The second measure is entirely silent, being filled by a whole-rest of four beats, but the time must be counted strictly during the silence, so that the four beats of silence in measure 2 take exactly the same amount of time as the four beats of sound in measure 1.

34

In measure 1, the half-note is sung for two beats, but the third and fourth beats are silent over the taps. The same is true in measure 2. Measure 3 is a familiar pattern of two half-notes which we have met several times before, and measure 4 is like the first two measures.

35

In each of the first two measures, the third quarter is silent. You must tap steadily, four beats to each measure beneath the sung tones, omitting the *Ta* each time on the third beat. Measure 3 is a pattern we have analyzed on page 20, consisting of a dotted half-note (held for three beats of the four) and a quarter-note for the fourth beat. The final measure has the same pattern we learned in the preceding exercise.

36

This one seems harder, but it won't hurt to try it. Measure 1 is really very similar to the first measure of the exercise before this, except that the first two beats are broken into eighth-notes instead of quarter-notes. You must sing two eighth-notes, *Ta-ta*, to each of the first two beats in the measure, remain silent on the third beat, and come in with a quarter-note for the fourth beat of the measure. Measure 2 is very much like measure 1, with this difference: that the second beat, instead of two eighth-notes, has one eighth-note and one eighth-rest. Instead of singing *Ta-ta Ta-ta* to the first two beats of measure 2, you must sing *Ta-ta Ta*, cutting off one eighth-note of sound for which an eighth-rest of silence has been substituted. Otherwise the two measures are the same. This pattern of omitting one eighth-note, just as you did it in measure 2, occurs twice in measure 3. Measure 4 has one long note of three beats in length, after which the last beat is silent.

Be sure to keep the underlying taps steady and even. If you find yourself interrupting these **tapped** beats or distorting them in any way to "humor" the difficulties of the rhythm, practice one measure at a time until you can do the exercise with strict, military precision.

You should make up more exercises of this sort for yourself.

TEMPO

37 It may already have occurred to you that the system we have been detailing is a *relative* system, not an absolute one.

We have indicated that a half-note is twice as long as a
quarter-note, and an eighth-note half as long as a quarter-
note, and we have tapped measures of four beats as yard-
sticks in measuring the lengths of the *Ta*s we have sung.
But how fast do we tap those beats? If you will check back
to the very beginning (page 1), you will notice that I arbi-
trarily instructed you to tap the beats "at about the speed
of a military march." But suppose you had tapped them at
the speed of a funeral march; then everything would have
been proportionately slower—the beats (and therefore the
quarter-notes) would have been slower, a half-note (since
it is double the value of a quarter-note) would have been
slower, and so on.

38   Clearly then, the whole structure depends upon the speed
at which the beats go by. The speed of the beats in a piece of
music is called the **tempo** (from the Italian word for "time"),
and it ordinarily is indicated at the beginning of a piece of
music by a word or a phrase of instructions. The composer
may say, "Fast," or "Very slowly," or "Moderately fast,
but with spirit," or something of the sort. Since this system
was spreading at a time when the Italians dominated the
musical world, it became customary for musicians of all
nations to use the Italian words for these instructions. There
are a great many of them in use and you will come across new
ones from time to time as your musical experience grows.
When you do, you'll have to look them up in a dictionary of
musical terms or an Italian-English dictionary, or ask a
musician who knows. The following table will cover a few
of the important ones, and a longer list is given at the end
of this book (Appendix II, page 156).

39   **SHORT TABLE of TEMPO INDICATIONS**
                                    FAST
Allegro—literally "happy," but now means fast even in
           Italian, when used in connection with music
Vivace—lively

Presto—very fast
Allegro con brio—fast, with brilliance
Allegro con spirito—fast, with spirit
MEDIUM
Andante—literally "going" or "walking" speed, i.e., neither
     running nor standing still, but moving moderately
Moderato—moderately
Allegretto—diminutive of *Allegro* (i.e., not so fast as *Allegro*)
SLOW
Lento—literally "slowly"
Grave—literally "heavily," or "seriously"
Adagio—literally "at ease"
Largo—literally "broadly"

40   The performing musician must use his judgment in de-
ciding just how fast is "Fast" and how slow is "Slow." Often
the nature of the piece makes this clear anyway. Most composers have been content to trust the singers or players in
this matter, but if they want to be absolutely sure that the
speed is clocked correctly, they can use the device known as
the **metronome.** The metronome is a kind of timepiece which
makes a ticking sound at any speed for which one sets it.
Metronome speeds are measured in beats per minute. If a
composer feels that he would like his music to move at the
rate of 60 beats per minute (one per second), he simply
writes at the beginning of the piece, ♩ = 60. This tells the
reader that each quarter-note is to move at the indicated
metronome speed; he can take his own metronome, set it at
60, and hear the correct speed ticked off by the instrument,
or he can gauge the speed fairly accurately with an ordinary
watch. Medium tempo, to most musicians, means somewhere
from 60 to 80 or 90 beats per minute; fast would be anything
above that; and slow anything below. (This is a very rough
demarcation, of course.) The United States Army Regula-
tions provide that troops are to march at a speed of 120
beats (or steps) per minute, and marches are always played

at that speed in the United States Army. That is, marches *for marching* are played at that speed; the same music might be played faster by the same band in a concert performance, where the music was being provided for listening rather than for marching. Circus bands and college football bands often play marches at faster speeds, too, in order to give a more brilliant or flashier effect.

You will find that, metronome or no metronome, musicians are always arguing about the "correct tempo" for a piece of music. And small wonder, for the composers themselves will tell you that the tempo which seems right one day may not seem so the next day. For most purposes, the verbal indications are accurate enough.

METER

41   There is another marking which you will find at the beginning of a piece of music. It is a set of two numbers, called the **metric signature** or **time signature.** They may be $\frac{2}{4}$ or $\frac{3}{4}$ or $\frac{4}{4}$ or $\frac{6}{8}$ or any of several other frequent combinations. They give you important information about the meter of a piece when you know how to read them. Before you can do this intelligently, it is necessary to look a little further into the nature of meter.

42   You will remember from the paragraph on this subject on page 4, that the steady pulse of the meter supplies a measuring stick for the more irregular rhythm of the piece of music itself. In each case we have tapped the steady beats of the meter, while we sang the particular rhythm of that piece. Now each piece has one meter which is most suitable for measuring it, just as for some given distance there would be one unit of measurement which would be more appropriate than others. For example, if you wanted to measure the width of an ordinary table, you would hardly think of doing it in miles; feet or inches would probably be more useful for most purposes. Theoretically, it would be possible to measure it in miles (it would be something like one two-thousandth of a mile, perhaps), but for most purposes there would be little use in doing so. On the other hand, if you were going to measure the distance from New York to Los Angeles, you probably *would* do it in miles; theoretically, again, you could do it in inches, but for most purposes the huge number of inches would be clumsy and inappropriate. Similarly, for a given melody, there is usually one meter which seems to fit better than others (a meter of four beats in the case of "Holy, Holy, Holy," for instance, – as you will remember from page 3 – and in most of the exercises we have been doing). You could force the melody, with some violence, into another meter, just as you could measure the width of the table in miles, but it would not seem so naturally suitable.

43 Now fortunately again for the simplification of our study, the number of meters used in most of our music is surprisingly small. *In fact, basically, there are only two or three important types of meters used in almost all the music of European civilization!* If you reflect that this includes symphonic music, operas, popular songs, jazz, most folk songs – almost all the music you are likely to encounter – it seems to be a pretty broad generalization, but it is essentially true. The principal meters are **Duple** (with two beats to each measure) and **Triple** (with three beats). Almost all others reduce to variants or combinations of these. Meters of fives, for instance, are relatively rare in music (despite the fact that the number 5 is so frequently used in our decimal numerical system). When meters of fives occur, they almost always are seen to boil down to combinations of the two basic meters (as 2+3, or as 3+2). Sixes are more frequent, but they are usually felt as two groups of threes, not as six real and separate beats. Similarly, nines reduce to three groups of threes.

Some readers may pounce on me with the reminder that in "Holy, Holy, Holy" (and, in fact, in most of the exercises so far) we have had a meter of fours. Yes, and some musicians do recognize this as a separate category. If it will make anyone happier, I'll concede the point, but to my ears even the fours tend to reduce to two groups of twos, as though we were counting **ONE**-two-*three*-four, with the heaviest beat on **ONE,** but a fairly heavy one also on *three.* But this is quibbling and not of basic importance to our study.

44   There have been many attempts, none of them completely satisfactory, to explain the tendency to rely on twos and threes in meter. Some people have suggested, for instance, that the duple, with its alternation of **HEAVY**-light, **HEAVY**-light, is related to biological processes: breathing for example, with its inhalation and exhalation; or the contraction and relaxation of the heart and blood vessels.

Others have pointed out that much music is associated with body movements. A march, for instance, is a functional piece of music, designed to accompany the movement of men from one place to another. Since human beings are equipped with two legs, the possibilities are rather limited. After a man has marched **LEFT**-right, he has in fact exhausted the possibilities and must begin over again, with another **LEFT**-right! Marches therefore *must* have two beats to a measure if they are to accomplish their purpose in the most direct manner, at least if they are marches for two-legged men. Presumably marches for the men from Mars, who may be blessed with five or six legs, might have five or six beats to a measure. Human beings, when their marches are written with six apparent beats, immediately group them into two groups of three each, and take one step to each *three* notes. (This happens with such favorites as "Washington Post" and "Semper Fidelis," by John Philip Sousa.)

In dancing, it is further suggested, the purpose of the movement is not entirely functional. To some extent it is decorative or recreational. Although twos are frequent in dancing, threes also appear. The waltz derives much of its charm from the fact that a creature with two legs is moving in a meter of three beats, so that a sequence of **LEFT**-right-left, **RIGHT**-left-right, **LEFT**-right-left is established, with a different leg beginning each measure, thus contributing to the lilt or shift of weight which is so characteristic of the dance.

These may be taken as speculations rather than as explanations. The student will decide for himself whether they help to cast light on the observed phenomena.

Now back to the **metric signature.**

45 Since the meter of a simple composition usually remains fixed for the length of the composition, it is possible and useful to indicate the nature of the measuring unit at the beginning of each piece. *The top number of the metric signature indicates how many beats there will be in each measure, and the bottom number indicates the value of each beat* (whether it is a quarter-note, a half-note, an eighth, et cetera). For example, a metric signature of $\frac{2}{4}$ (read "two-four time" or "two-quarter time") means that each measure of the piece will have two beats, and that each beat will be a quarter-note. A signature of $\frac{3}{4}$ (read "three-four time" or "three-quarter time") means that each measure will have three beats, and that each beat will be a quarter-note. A signature of $\frac{4}{4}$ (read "four-four time" or "four-quarter time") means that each measure will have four beats, and that each beat will be a quarter-note. A signature of $\frac{3}{2}$ (read "three-two time" or "three-half time") means that each measure will have three beats, and each beat will be a *half*-note.

RHYTHM PATTERNS

46 Now the student must understand that a piece of music in $\frac{2}{4}$ *meter* need not have the same *rhythm* of two quarter-notes in every measure. The only requirement is that the notes and rests in each measure *add up to a value of two quarter-notes*. There are thousands and thousands of possible combinations of the symbols we have been learning. The meter requires a total of two quarter-notes in each measure of $\frac{2}{4}$ time, and of three quarter-notes in each measure of $\frac{3}{4}$ time, but the rhythm of each piece will divide up the time between the bar lines in many ways.

For example, here are some characteristic combinations which you might find in a piece of music in $\frac{2}{4}$ time. In each case, the notes and rests between the bar lines of a measure will add up to the equivalent of two quarter-notes:

Some Characteristic Rhythms in $\frac{2}{4}$ Meter

47   Try each of them. The best way is to sing the particular rhythm with the syllable *Ta* as we have done before, while you tap the basic two beats at the same time. For instance:

You tap two beats, **"ONE**-two." While you tap the first beat, you sing a *Ta* of the same length as the beat, but while you tap the second beat, you sing *Ta-ta* to make the two eighth-notes. When you have it right, do about four of these measures, one after the other, so that you establish firmly in your mind the sound of the rhythm which is printed:

The result will be:

48   Try the next one: . While you tap the two regular beats, you will sing just one long *Ta* which lasts as long as both beats together.

49   The next one:

Here, of course, you do on both beats what you did only on the second beat in Section 47.

50   The next:

This is a little trickier. The measure includes a dotted quarter-note and an eighth-note. This means that the first note is really held for a quarter plus an eighth — 1½ beats — after which the second note gets only half a beat. In other words, as you tap evenly, **ONE**-two, the dotted quarter-note will sound not only for all of "**ONE**," but also for half of "two." Then the eighth-note will get the remaining half of the "two."

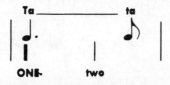

If you have any trouble getting the feel of such fractions of beats, here is a good way to solve the problem. Mentally subdivide each beat into two halves by thinking "**ONE**-*and*-two-*and*," with the number getting only half of each beat and the syllable *"and"* getting the other half of it. The taps must be kept exactly the same speed as before, and you still must think "**ONE**-two" with them as they go by, but you add lightly between beats the extra syllable *"and."* Like this:

ONE- and-two- and

When you can do this, you have only to observe that the rhythm of our measure requires notes on "**ONE**," and on the *"and"* after "two." It is as though you started strongly on **ONE**, held the first note lightly during *"and*-two," and sounded out again on the *"and"* after "two."

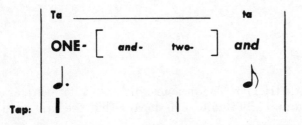

Do it over and over until it makes sense and comes easily to you:

The eighth-note will always come *after* the second tap in each measure.

51 The last combination involves a quarter-rest: | 𝄽 ♩ |. Here you sing nothing on the first beat, but put a *Ta* squarely on the second beat.

52 Here is a line of music which uses all these different ²⁄₄ combinations together, plus a new one at the end:

Try it as though it were a melody. Keep the taps steady and even, and sing the *Ta*s above them as the notation calls for them. The last two measures are tied together, forming one long note which must therefore be held for four beats.

53   Here are some additional combinations which you should practice.

It will be good experience to work them out for yourself, but here are some suggestions and hints:

In the first measure, not only is each beat divided in half, but the *"and"* of "two" is itself divided into two halves, forming sixteenth-notes.

In measure 2, the first beat is divided into four sixteenth-notes by the same process so that you must sing four fast *Ta*s in the time of that one beat; the second beat of that measure has only one short *Ta*, because you are asked to leave an eighth-note of silence on the *"and"* of "two." (There would be a slight difference of effect if this measure were written: ,

with a quarter-note filling all of the second beat. Try it both ways, singing accurately, to understand the difference.)

The first half of measure 3 is the same as the first half of measure 2; but the second part of the measure introduces a new combination—a dotted eighth plus a sixteenth:

There are several ways to learn to sing this accurately. One is to remember how the four sixteenths sounded on the first beat of the measure, and then to hold the dotted eighth for the value of three of them, leaving one for the final sixteenth:

Another is to observe that this notation does the same thing as ♩. ♪

(which we worked out before), only twice as fast: that is, just as the eighth-note in ♩. ♪

comes just after the second beat, so does the sixteenth-note in ♩. ♪

come after the *"and"* of the second beat.

The last measure has one sound which fills the first beat, and a silence on the second beat. (Test the difference between

| ♩ 𝄾 ‖

and

| ♩ ‖

as an ending.)

When you have learned these separately, try them as a continuous line of music, repeating them until everything is thoroughly under control.

54 On pages 39 to 44 are some patterns in $\frac{3}{4}$ meter and $\frac{4}{4}$ meter which you must work out so that you can read them

with ease. *Don't skip this step,* even if it seems obvious and
self-evident to you. If you do, you will have only a theoretical
knowledge of this part of the reading of music and there
will be no practical foundation on which to build additional
skill. This practice is the equivalent of learning multiplica-
tion tables in arithmetic; you have to *memorize* some of the
standard combinations in musical notation so that they
become tools with which you can work in reading more complicated pieces of music. In arithmetic you memorize, for
example, that 3 x 5 is 15, so that you can use this information
in any larger problem which involves 3 x 5. If, in the middle
of an advanced problem, you had to sit down and put together
three sets of five ∷∷∷and then count the units to determine how many they were, your work would be continually
held back by wasting time on such elementary matters. Similarly in music, you must have the most frequent combinations down pat so that you can use them promptly and
without hesitation when necessary.

Directions for Working Exercises on Pages 39 to 41

55   *Use the same method that we used on page 32 for the* $\frac{2}{4}$
*meter: Take each measure separately at first, tap the three
beats of the measure,* **ONE**-*two-three, and sing on the syllable* Ta. *When you are sure that you have it right, do about
four repetitions of the measure, one after the other, until
you associate clearly in your mind a certain rhythmic sound
with the printed pattern.*

*For example, taking No. 1 from the list of patterns on
page 39, work it out as follows:*

Then do four of these in a row:

56 *Then do the same thing with each of the other sample measures. As you do each one, try to observe similarities to those you have already solved so that you avoid needless duplication of effort.*

57 Some Characteristic Rhythms in ¾ Meter

Obviously No. 3 is just a slight variant of No. 1 — the last beat is divided into two eighth-notes, but otherwise the pattern is the same.

Notice that No. 12 and No. 13 are two ways of writing the same thing; the only difference is that the notation of No. 13 makes you think of the tones as grouped in a slightly different way from the grouping of No. 12, but the rhythmic values are identical.

No. 14 is solved in the same way as the $\frac{2}{4}$ dotted rhythm which we did on page 33, Section 50; the only change is the addition of a third beat to the measure (after the dotted rhythm).

No. 15 is based on the same principle as No. 14, only this time the extra quarter-note is in front of the dotted pattern which, therefore, is spread over the last two beats of the measure instead of the first two beats.

No. 16 is a slight variant of No. 14.

No. 17 is a slight variant of No. 15.

Compare No. 24 with No. 17.

Compare No. 26 with both No. 24 and No. 17.

58   When you feel quite comfortable with these separate measures, try the following exercises, which combine such measures into continuous rhythms:

59   Next, work the following problems in $\frac{4}{4}$ meter, using methods similar to those described on page 38, Section 55 (but tapping four beats to a measure, of course, instead of three).

60   **Some Characteristic Rhythms in $\frac{4}{4}$ Meter**

Notice the relationship between No. 11 and No. 13; then compare this with No. 15.

Notice that No. 25 and No. **26 are** identical except in the way of indicating the grouping.

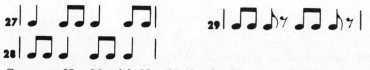

Compare No. 28 with No. 29; in the former, the **second** and the **fourth beats** are quarters; in **the latter, they are** eighths, with an eighth-rest.

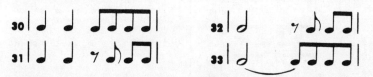

Notice the slight difference in effect between No. 33 and No. 32.

Observe the slight differences as **you** change from No. 34, to 35, to 36.

39. | 𝅗𝅥   𝅘𝅥.   ♪ | 41. | 𝅗𝅥 ♫♫ 𝅘𝅥 | 𝅗𝅥 |

40. | 𝅘𝅥 ♫♪ 𝄾 ♪𝅘𝅥 | 42. | 𝅗𝅥 ♫♫ 𝅘𝅥 | 𝅗𝅥 |

Observe the slight differences as you go from No. 41 to 42;
then compare 45 with them.

43. | ♫♫♫♫ 𝅗𝅥 𝅗𝅥 | 44. | ♪ 𝄾 𝄾 ♫𝅘𝅥 𝅗𝅥 |

Observe the relationship between No. 44 and No. 36.

45. | 𝅗𝅥 𝄾 ♫♫𝅘𝅥 𝅗𝅥 |

Nos. 46, 47, and 48 represent a series, too:

46. | 𝅗𝅥 𝅘𝅥.♫𝅘𝅥.♫𝅘𝅥 | 49. | 𝅗𝅥 ♫♫♫♫𝅘𝅥 𝅗𝅥 |
                                              3   3

47. | 𝅗𝅥 𝅘𝅥𝄾𝅘𝅥𝄾𝅘𝅥 | 50. | 𝅗𝅥 𝅗𝅥 𝅗𝅥|𝅗𝅥 𝅗𝅥 𝅗𝅥|𝅗𝅥 etc.

48. | 𝅗𝅥 ♫𝄾𝄾♫𝄾𝄾𝅘𝅥 |

Practice the tied notes in No. 50 carefully.

51. | 𝅗𝅥 𝅗𝅥 ♫𝅘𝅥|𝅗𝅥 ♫𝅘𝅥𝅘𝅥 𝄾 ‖

For a detailed explanation of No. 51, see Section 61, which
follows immediately after this table.

61   The last exercise, No. 51, introduces some combinations
which are called **syncopations**. A syncopated tone begins *just
before the beat* and is tied over into the beat and sometimes
after it. For instance, the note which is tied over the bar line
between the two measures above, begins just before the first

beat of measure 2 and is held over into that beat:

It gives almost the effect of anticipating the beat, of rushing in impatiently, as though the real intention might have been

but the first beat of measure 2 got started a little bit too soon. Notice that without the tie, there would be no syncopation:

for the first beat of measure 2 would then have a new tone beginning on it in the usual way, and there would be no question of a tone held over from before the beat. Similarly, in the middle of measure 2, it is the tie which makes the pleasant effect of the last note coming a bit too soon. Here it anticipates the third beat instead of the first, but the principle is the same. Try singing *Ta*s to this rhythm,

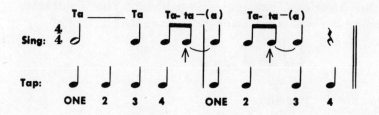

being sure that you *don't* sing another *ta* on the second part of the syncopated note, but merely hold over the "*a*" of the **ta** _____ which began just before the beat.

Syncopations may occur with respect to any beat of a measure and in any meter:

sometimes written:

Even the *"and"* of a beat may have syncopations:

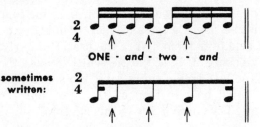

In American jazz the syncopation of one eighth-note before the beat is especially common so that instead of

you are likely to find

almost as the norm.

OTHER METERS

62   The most common meters are $\frac{2}{4}$, $\frac{3}{4}$, and $\frac{4}{4}$,* as you might guess from our earlier discussion of meter on pages 29 ff. Sometimes, however, you will see metric signatures of $\frac{2}{2}$ $\frac{3}{2}$, and $\frac{4}{2}$ indicating that there are 2, 3, and 4 beats, respectively, but that each beat is a *half*-note instead of a quarter.

Let's look at this aspect for a moment. Since the speed of the beats varies with the tempo marking of the piece *(Allegro, Andante,* etc.), as we have seen on page 26, isn't it possible that a slow quarter-note may be the same as a fast half-note? Suppose, for instance, that we have a composition in $\frac{3}{4}$ meter, and the composer has marked it *"Lento,* ♩ = 40";

and suppose we have another composition in $\frac{3}{2}$ meter, which the composer has labeled *"Allegro,* ♩ = 120."

The half-note beat of the second example actually would be *faster* than the quarter-note beat of the first example! This happens very often in music, and the truth of the matter is that the choice of quarter-notes or half-notes as the unit for the beat is not a matter of tremendous difference and depends to some extent on the personal whim of the composer. The difference is chiefly psychological: a fast piece in $\frac{3}{4}$ meter will tend to have lots of sixteenth-notes and thirty-second-notes and therefore will look "blacker" than the same piece written in $\frac{3}{2}$ meter, where eighth-notes would

---

*A large **C** is sometimes used as a symbol for $\frac{4}{4}$ time. This is not, as some popular manuals will misinform you, because the **C** stands for "common time," but because a circle was used in the Middle Ages to represent triple time, and a broken circle to represent duple time. Triple time was called "perfect" time by the Church musicians because it suggested the Trinity, and it therefore was symbolized by the circle which is perfect in that it is endless; the broken circle represented "imperfect" or duple time.

take the place of the sixteenths, sixteenth-notes would re-
place the thirty-seconds, and so on. Therefore the $\frac{3}{2}$ notation
might give the performer a more placid or less intense
impression than the $\frac{3}{4}$ Some composers seem to prefer the
open look of half-note beats (Sibelius, for example) and
some the tighter look of the quarter-note beats. Here is an
example: On page 42 we had a rhythm in $\frac{3}{4}$ meter which
looked like this:

This rhythm could be written just as well in $\frac{3}{2}$ meter, as
follows:

They may look different on paper, but if the half-note beat
of the second one is taken at the same speed as the quarter-
note beat of the first one, they will sound identical. This
actually occurs quite frequently: you are as likely to see a
piece marked $\s</em>d = 90$, as you are to see it marked $\downarrow = 90$.
Here is another example of the same thing: On page 36,
we had a rhythm in $\frac{2}{4}$ meter, which looked like this:

Here is the same effect achieved by writing it in $\frac{2}{2}$ meter:

In fact, meters of $\frac{3}{8}$ and $\frac{3}{16}$ are also quite frequent; they are triple meters, like $\frac{3}{4}$ and $\frac{3}{2}$ but the eighth-note and sixteenth are used as their unit beats instead of the quarter or half. These meters, of course, will give an even "blacker" look since they will tend to use thirty-second- and sixty-fourth-notes. Beethoven liked to use them for his slow pieces, where the "black" look was really deceptive, since the eighth or sixteenth was actually moving at a slow speed.

63   Sometimes ordinary $\frac{4}{4}$ is taken so fast that the half-note feels like the unit instead of the quarter. In such cases, it should really be written as $\frac{2}{2}$ meter, but some composers don't bother to make the differentiation.*

COMPOUND METERS

64   When the basic beats of the principal meters are subdivided into triplets, a whole family of **compound meters** is born. For instance, if each beat in $\frac{2}{4}$ meter is subdivided into three equal parts, we have $\frac{6}{8}$ meter.

*Occasionally, just as the **C** is used for $\frac{4}{4}$ time, the sort of **fast** $\frac{4}{4}$ in which the half-note is taken as the unit is represented by the symbol **₵** . This is called "cut time" and, as suggested above, is really the same as $\frac{2}{2}$. Once in a while the Italian phrase *alla breve* ("by the half-note") is printed at the beginning instead of the **₵** , to accomplish the same result.

As hinted before, on page 30, $^6_8$ meter, therefore, is really
a duple meter with a subdivsion on each of the two basic
beats. It is only when the $^6_8$ is taken at an extremely slow
tempo that each of the six beats is felt separately as important, and even then the fourth beat usually feels heavier than
the fifth and sixth, as though it were the beginning of an
important sub-group.

Fast $^6_8$ ("Pop! Goes the Weasel") :

Slow $^6_8$ ("Silent Night") :

Note that the bracket and the number 3 need not be written
over the triplets in $^6_8$ meter; they can be taken for granted,
since the whole point of establishing the $^6_8$ was to permit the
use of such triplets as a fundamental part of a meter.

Similarly, $^9_8$ meter can be formed by subdividing each beat
of $^3_4$ into a triplet.

And $\frac{12}{8}$ can be formed from $\frac{4}{4}$ by the same process.

This means that a composer, if he knows that he will be using triplets as a regular part of the rhythmic structure of his piece, may write in $\frac{12}{8}$ or $\frac{9}{8}$, instead of $\frac{4}{4}$ or $\frac{3}{4}$, and thereby not only avoid the trouble and time of constantly bracketing groups of notes with 3s, but also make it immediately clear to the reader that the triplet subdivision is characteristic of that particular piece.

("Beautiful Dreamer," Stephen Foster)

("Royal Fireworks Music," G. F. Händel)

EXERCISES: READING RHYTHMS

65   This really sums up most of what you must know about the notation of rhythm! There are a few other details which will be introduced toward the end of the book as they occur in special problems. But meanwhile, I think you will be surprised to find that the rhythms of many well-known tunes are actually much easier to read than the exercises you have already succeeded in doing. For instance, here is the rhythmic pattern of "Yankee Doodle."

It should be a snap for you. Sing the top line, using the syllable *Ta* for each written note, according to our system, while you tap the two regular beats in each measure.

Here is the beginning of "America" ("My Country, 'Tis of Thee") with the meter beats indicated beneath the rhythmic notation. You should try it in the same way, singing *Ta* to each symbol.

The second and fourth measures have the rhythm of dotted quarter plus eighth which should be familiar to you by now. The rest is as easy as they come.

Here is the beginning of "Jingle Bells."

Sing it with the syllable *Ta,* but first write in the beats to be tapped beneath the given notes.

"Jingle Bells" could also have been written in cut time, **₵** , or in ²⁄₂. The only difference would be that all the note values would *look* twice as large as in the ²⁄₄ version, although they would *sound* the same if the beat were tapped at the same speed (regardless of whether it were a quarter-note or a half-note) :

66 Try the following familiar examples. They represent the rhythmic patterns of well-known melodies. However, sing them with the syllable *Ta,* and all on one tone — without the melodic line — even if you know the words and the correct tune. In other words, sing exactly what is notated here so that you get the practice of reading rhythms from printed notes, which is the whole point of these exercises.* Before you begin each one, look at the metric signature, and then tap the proper number of beats in each measure as you sing. Also be sure to observe the tempo indications, so that you are tapping at the correct speed.

*Sometimes several different versions exist for a single hymn or folk tune. Such tunes tend to change as they pass through new hands and are adapted to new texts—especially if they are transmitted orally instead of being written down. If you notice such variants for any of the examples used in the following pages, try to analyze wherein they differ from the version given here.

1. "Reuben and Rachel" ("Reuben, Reuben")

Allegro

2. "Joy To The World"

Notice that measures 9 and 10 are repeated in measures 11 and 12; and that 13 and 14 are repeated in 15 and 16. Catching such repetitions will save you much work.

Allegro

3. "Come Thou Almighty King"

Look for the repetitions of the two-measure phrases beginning in measure 9.

Moderato

4. "Santa Lucia"

Each half of this piece is repeated in performance; that is, the first eight measures are sung and repeated immediately, then the last eight are sung and repeated.

Andante

5. "Oh, What a Beautiful Morning" (Rodgers)

Waltz tempo

6. "Onward, Christian Soldiers"

Keep the beats steady and marchlike.

Allegro

7. "Holy, Holy, Holy, Lord God Almighty"

Moderato

8. "Hark, the Herald Angels Sing"

Notice that the first eight measures are really just four measures which are repeated; and that the last eight divide into two groups of four which are very similar to each other.

Allegro ma non troppo

9. "All Through the Night"

Notice that the first four measures, the next four, and the last four, all have the same rhythmic pattern; it is only measures 9 to 12 which are different!

Lento

10. "Frère Jacques"

Allegro

11. "Smoke Gets in Your Eyes" (Kern)

Slowly

12. "Old Folks at Home" (Swanee River)

The first eight measures of this song are usually sung twice in actual performance, but instrumentalists sometimes skip the repetition when they play the music without words.

The only tricky rhythm is the one which occurs in the second half of measures 2, 6, and 14. It is a slight syncopation, in which the last note of the measure occupies not only

the last beat but also an eighth before it, as is clearly seen
from the alternate notation given with those measures.

Andante

13. "Drink to Me Only with Thine Eyes"
Notice that measures 1-4, 5-8, and 13-16 are essentially
repetitions. Only 9-12 is a different pattern.

Andante (six beats per measure)

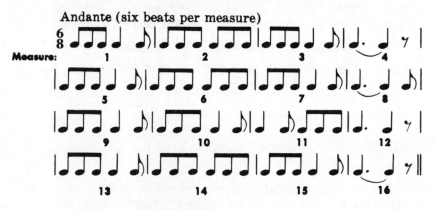

14. "Three Blind Mice"
In $\frac{6}{8}$, a note which fills a whole measure should be written

$\left|\begin{smallmatrix} \end{smallmatrix}\right.$ ♩. ♩. | . But sometimes you will find it written | ♩. | instead. It is true that they add up to the same number of eighths, but the first way is more appropriate to the duple nature of $\frac{6}{8}$ meter and is really more correct.

Allegro molto vivace (two fast beats per measure)

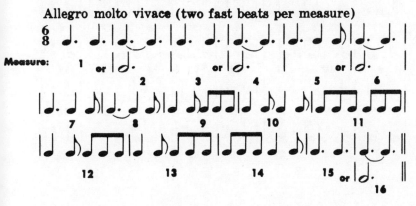

15. "Deck the Halls"

This one also has the familiar scheme of a four-measure phrase repeated immediately and then once again at the very end, with four different measures for contrast or variety just before the last group. Notice that there are only two beats to a measure (each half-note gets a beat), since this piece is written in cut time. It will sound the same as $\frac{2}{4}$ time.

Allegro

16. "People Will Say We're in Love" (Rodgers)
In performance, the first sixteen measures are repeated.

Moderato

17. "Blue Skies" (Berlin)

Moderato

67 You should experiment by making up new patterns of notes and rests in different meters, especially in the common meters such as $\frac{2}{4}$, $\frac{3}{4}$, $\frac{4}{4}$, and $\frac{6}{8}$. Make up some as separate measures, and others as complete lines of music. Then read them back to yourself with the syllable *Ta*, tapping the correct beat at the same time.

68 WARNING: Don't go on to the next subject until you can do all the exercises in this section with ease. If it doesn't work the first time, don't be impatient or discouraged and you'll find that after a few tries everything will fall into line.

PART TWO

Notation of Pitch

The second part of this study will be easier for you if you understand a few details about the physical nature of sound. Go along with me on the following little experiment and try to imagine that you are actually doing it at the same time — or, if you feel ambitious, get a piece of string and a pencil and really perform the experiment. It's very simple, but very important.

69 Take a piece of strong but thin string about eight or ten feet long (not rope, which would be too stiff and heavy for our purpose), and fasten one end of it securely to a fixed object — a door-knob or door-hinge will do, or one of those rods inside a closet, or a heavy piece of furniture that won't move when you pull on the string. Now tie the loose end around a pencil. Using the pencil as a handle or grip in your left hand, pull the string taut. Pluck the string with your other hand as though it were a big fiddle-string and listen for the deep tone it produces.

Now pull as hard as you can on the pencil with your left hand, and pluck the string again with your right. You will find that the sound produced by the tightened string is a little higher than the first one.

Next, roll more of the string around the pencil so that only about three feet of string remains exposed, and try to pull it just as tight as you did the first time. Pluck it, and you will observe that the sound produced is noticeably higher and shriller than for the longer string!

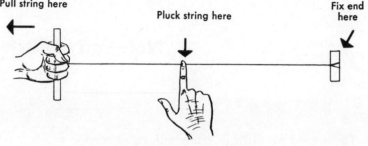

Pull string here

Pluck string here

Fix end here

LONG STRING, LOW SOUND

Pull here

Pluck here

Fixed end

SHORTENED STRING, HIGHER SOUND

A little experimenting on your own will convince you that you can accomplish this raising of the pitch by either of two methods: shortening the string, or pulling it tighter. What do these two methods have in common that causes them both to raise the pitch of the vibrating string?

70   A check, easily performed in any physics or acoustics laboratory, reveals that in both cases the frequency of vibration (i.e., the number of vibrations per second) goes up. In other words, *the pitch of a vibrating string*—how low or high it sounds — *depends upon the number of vibrations per second.* For a given number of vibrations, the same sound will always be produced. If the string is shortened (or tightened), a higher number of vibrations and therefore a higher pitch is produced. If it is lengthened (or slackened), a lower pitch is produced.

71   We find that when a string is divided exactly in half (keeping the tightness constant) a pitch results which bears such a close resemblance to the original one that many people mistake one for the other, and even trained listeners must grant the "family" resemblance. If we name the first tone A, then we might call the next one A^1, perhaps, to show that it is similar, although not exactly the same. What is more, common sense makes us suspect that if we were to start with the *half* string, and divide *it* in half, the same thing would happen once more. That is, another tone would be produced, higher than the half-string's tone, but bearing the same family resemblance to it, in turn. Experiment shows that this process can indeed be repeated indefinitely, producing a whole series of As (A^1, A^2, A^3, A^4, A^5, etc.) as we continue to divide each half in half again.

In the same way, if we take another length of string instead of the length which produced the first A — let's call the new one B — a whole new family of tones, different from the A family, but related to each other, is formed. We can name the new series B^1, B^2, B^3, etc.

72   All this information, and much more, was known as early as the time of Pythagoras, 500 years before the Christian Era. Early theoreticians, therefore, in naming the tones used in music, used the method of calling all tones of the same family by the same letter-name, as we have just done. It was found necessary to use only seven different letter-names, since the eighth tone, when it was reached, turned out to be

the familiar one produced by half of the string which gave
the first tone. In other words, if the different tones were
named A B C D E F G the next one in line would not need a
new letter-name since it would be the A^1 which we obtained
by dividing A in half. The whole system would look like this:
A B C D E F G A^1 B^1 C^1 D^1 E^1 F^1 G^1 A^2 B^2 C^2 D^2 E^2
F^2 G^2 .... and so on.

It must be admitted that A^1 and A^2 are not the same tone
as A (since they have different frequencies) but it is useful
to call them by the same letter-name so that the musical
"alphabet" can be kept at a manageable size. Imagine how
cumbersome it would be if each tone really had a separate
name which, moreover, would not suggest the close relationship that each eighth tone bears to the one below it with
the same letter-name. The eighth tone above any given tone
—the one corresponding to half its string length — is called
its **octave** (from the Latin word for "eighth").

EARLY NOTATION METHODS

73   Little is known about the actual sound of ancient Greek
music, but we do know that Greek musical notation used
letter-names to indicate the pitch. The method was to write
the desired pitch-name above the word or syllable to which
it was sung. For example, if, in a hymn to Helios, the name
of the god was to be sung to the tones A C B (for simplicity,
let's use our own alphabet, instead of the Greek) it was sufficient to write those letter-names above the syllables of the
sung word: A   C   B
           HE – LI – OS
Since the rhythm of Greek vocal music was inseparable
from the rhythm of the poetry with which it was combined,
this notation was adequate, for the reader knew the rhythm
of the words and needed only the pitch indications given by
the letters written above the words.

74   This system of notation has been carried over into ours
to the extent that we, too, use letter-names for the various

tones. But in other ways it was not a satisfactory sy~
for it was difficult to combine it with the rhythmic notation
which we have described in the first part of this book. A way
had to be found to combine in one symbol the indications
of both rhythm and pitch.

In the Middle Ages a system was in use in some parts of
Europe which had the possibilities of such a notation in it.
In some monasteries, when a group of monks was to sing
together, one of them, acting as leader, would indicate by
the rising and falling of his hand the general direction of
the melody. For example, if he wished to show the melodic
fragment we have used above for the word "HELIOS," he
might move his hand thus:

(A)   (C)   (B)

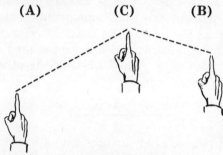

This permitted only an approximation, of course (how high
above A, for instance, must one move the hand for C?), but
it was perfectly adequate as a reminder for singers who
really knew the melodies and merely needed to have their
memories refreshed a bit. The system which included this
device was known as "chironomy," from the Greek words
for "hand" and "sign."

75   It was natural, when these musicians wanted to write
down their melodies, that they should evolve a notation
which was suggested by the patterns made by the leader's
hand. This notation, the "neumes," is reminiscent of the path

followed by the hand in chironomy. The little fragment used above might have been represented in this fashion: ⌒⌃

later becoming: ⌒⌒

But it was still an approximation. How high above the starting point did one have to go to indicate C? There was no fixed standard to answer this question.

76   The great revolution in musical notation, the idea which solved this problem, came with an invention which was as important to music as the wheel to general civilization. Yet it is so simple that one finds it hard to believe that its discovery had to wait so long. It was not until the tenth century of the Christian Era that some genius thought of drawing *a horizontal line to act as a point of reference!** If it were agreed that the horizontal line represented A, for example, one could see at a glance whether the other pitches were higher or lower than A.

A   ⎯⎯⎯⎯⌒⌒⎯⎯⎯⎯

Yet even this was only an approximation after all, for until some unit or standard of measuring distances from A was introduced, there was still no indication of how far above A one should sing in the fragment represented above.

77   It seems to have taken almost a century more before another unsung genius thought of the touch which finally made the system secure — the adding of a second line! For

*The credit for this discovery is often given to Guido d'Arezzo, but it is far from certain that he deserves it. Guido got the credit for a dozen things that were done within 200 years of either side of his life span! Mankind likes to pile all the glory on one hero, as it does all the blame on one scapegoat.

now, if one said that the distance from A to C, for instance, was to be represented by the distance between the two lines,

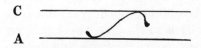

not only were those two tones definitely fixed in notation, but the tone between them (B) could be identified by going only half the distance between them, and all the other tones eventually could be shown by marking off the same standard distance. For the sake of economy, the spaces between the lines were used for names of tones as well as the lines themselves (as we have just suggested for B). The great advantage of the lines, from a historical viewpoint, was that it was easy to combine their indications of pitch with the rhythmic notation, merely by setting the desired rhythmic symbol on the appropriate line or space.

78   Once this was appreciated, more lines were added in the writing of music so that all the notes were provided with lines or spaces.* In fact, for a while Europe went line-crazy. I have seen examples as late as the sixteenth century, in which the number of lines was dizzying — sometimes eleven or more:

*For the sake of historical accuracy, it should be stated that the first line tried in the tenth century was a line for F; then one for C was added, and later one for A. We have introduced them in a slightly different order in the last few paragraphs so that the student could judge their usefulness in connection with the simple melodic fragment (A C B) which we had been discussing.

Some of the lines had to be labeled with their letter-names as reminders, since the eye could not always grasp their identity among so many. But it would have been absurd to have carried this to the point of labeling all lines, since this would have taken us back to the letter system from which we started, and the very purpose of the line method would have been wasted.

79   The solution of this problem was a compromise. One line was removed in the middle of a series of eleven, so that *two* groups of five each remained.

Notice how this helps: The reader now has two compact sets of lines which can be sized up at a glance. He can identify as "the bottom line of the upper five," or "the top line of the lower five" a note which formerly would have been lost somewhere in the middle of the whole confusing series. It is visually and psychologically more practical.

80   If the middle line — the one that was removed — is needed to represent that particular note, a small piece of it can be written in:

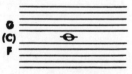

In this way, we provide a line on which to write the desired note, without destroying the effect of separating the two groups.

THE STAFF

81   This is essentially the system we use today. Each group
of five lines is called a **staff**. (The plural is "staves.") For
high voices, like sopranos, and for high instruments, like
flutes or violins, it is customary to use just the upper staff;
the other notes would be too low for them to sing or play
anyway. For instruments like the double-bass or tuba, of
course, the lower staff is more useful. The piano, and a few
other instruments which are regularly required to play both
high and low notes at the same time, read from the full
double staff, sometimes called the *Great Staff*.

CLEFS

82   On each staff, one line is always marked with a symbol
for its letter-name. The upper staff uses a symbol derived
from the Gothic letter *G* (it still looks very much like a *G)*
and its tail is always wrapped around the correct line for
the note G:

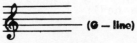

The lower staff uses a symbol derived from the letter *F*.
Originally it looked like this:

𝄐 .

This degenerated to

𝄢 ,

and finally the arms of the *F* became just dots; but those
two dots are always placed so that the correct line for F
is between them:

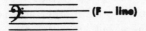

These letter symbols are called **clefs**, from the French word for "key," because they act as keys to the identities of the lines and spaces.*

The F clef is sometimes called the **bass clef** (pronounced "base" but spelled "bass"), because it is used for the low voices and instruments. The G clef is sometimes called the **treble clef** because the high voice which uses it was once known as the "treble" or "triple" (i.e., "third" voice, counting up).

83   Let's try some sample cases to learn the meaning of **the** clefs.

Suppose you are asked the name of the following note:

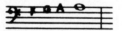

You know that the line between the two dots is F. But the note is in the space above that line. Therefore, it must be the next higher letter-name, G.

84   Look at the note above the G:

Here you must remember that in music we use only the letters A, B, C, D, E, F, and G. Therefore, the next higher note above G is an A.

*Sometimes the middle line (the C that was removed) is labeled with a clef derived from the old form of the letter *C*, but this is much rarer nowadays than the G and F, and you really don't have to bother with it unless you are going to read very old music, or music for full orchestra or for certain other ensembles. For this reason, it is not included here, but an explanation of it is given at the end of the book (Appendix III, p. 163) for those who are interested.

85   If the given note is below the clef line, you must simply count back in the alphabet as you go down. For instance:

To reach this note, you must **count down** below the F line. The space below that line is **E, and the** next line below (which is the one we want) must **therefore** be D.

86   For the G clef, you use the **same** method, counting up or down from G. Always remember to count from the correct letter according to the clef, and to count spaces as well as lines as you go up or down through the musical alphabet of seven letter-names. Let's take an example in the G clef:

The second line from the bottom is the one we know to be G; so we can count up to the note we wish to identify. Simply count each space and line as you go up, remembering that the musical alphabet starts over again after G. Very well, we have:

and the note in question comes out F.

EXERCISES: IDENTIFYING NOTES

87   With a little practice, you will find that it is not necessary to count each time. After all, there are not so many lines and spaces, and you will soon have the "look" of each note memorized.Try writing whole-notes (like those we have been reading) on different lines and spaces of each staff and naming

them, just for the sake of practice. Here is a batch to begin
with*:

LEGER LINES

88   The note which sits on top of the upper staff is G, as you
can verify for yourself. The note just below the staff is D:

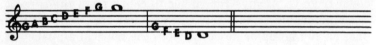

Suppose we want to write a note higher than G or lower
than D, for which there is no line provided? The method
is simple and logical: we just write in a small piece of line
where it is needed, as we did for the line between the two
staves (page 70):

89   For still higher notes, or lower ones, we have only to add
more of these pieces of line:

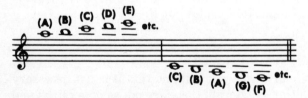

To the strong of will: The letter-names of these notes are given
on page 169, but don't look at them until you have solved each
case for yourself.

90 The same process may be used with the lower staff:

The small pieces of line are known as **"leger lines."** Practice writing and reading them until you can identify them instantly.

ACCIDENTALS

91 But the account is not yet complete. In addition to the tones represented by the letters from A to G, a few other tones were introduced into the system as time went by. The story of how and why this happened is a complicated one, but fortunately you can learn to read the notes without going into their ancient history. Later, if you are curious about it, you can delve into the historical side of the matter. For the present, let us simplify it by saying that an attempt was made to sandwich new tones between some of the existing ones — a tone between F and G, another between G and A, another between A and B, et cetera. This embarrassed the system; no allowance had been made for these extra notes when it was evolved. Between A and B there obviously is no other letter available, and between a line and the space above it there is no room on the staff for the notation of an extra note. A compromise was effected. The method that was worked out was to think of the tone between A and B either as "A raised" or "B lowered," the tone between F and G either as "F raised" or "G lowered," and so on. Instead of the word "raised," we say **sharp** in music, and instead of "lowered" we say **flat.** *F-sharp,* then, is a tone midway between F and G, and it can just as correctly be called *G-flat.* Similarly, the tone between A and B can be called either A-sharp or B-flat.

92 To write these new notes on the staff, symbols were needed

to take the place of the words "sharp" and "flat." The symbol
for sharp is written ♯ (something like a tic-tac-toe frame),
and the symbol for flat is written ♭ (something like a small
letter *b*, from which, indeed, it is derived). Symbols which
alter the pitch in this way are called **accidentals.** Although
we put the accidentals *after* the letter-name when we speak
or write in words, we put them *before* the notes to which
they refer when we write music on a staff so that the music
reader is warned of the approach of a modified form of the
tone:

Notice how the tone between F and G can assume two forms:
either F♯ or G♭; and the tone between G and A two forms:
either G♯ or A♭.

THE PIANO KEYBOARD

Now let us relate what we know to the keyboard of a
piano. In this way we will be able to find on the keyboard
the meaning of the notes we read and actually translate them

The Piano

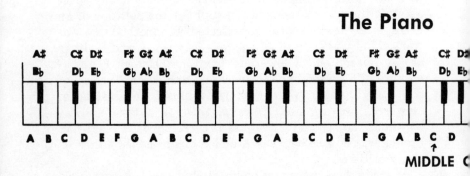

into sound. As you read the following pages, compare them as often as possible with the keyboard of a real piano or with the diagram of a keyboard shown below.

93 The white keys on the piano represent the letter-names from A to G, without any accidentals. The black keys are the sharps and flats, sandwiched between the others. Each black key has two names — F♯ and G♭, for instance, or A♯ and B♭.

94 You will notice that the black keys are arranged in alternating groups of two and three, separated by gaps — a group of three, a gap, a group of two, another gap, and so on, over and over again.

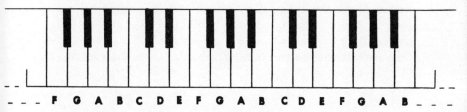

There is a very good reason for this. The distances in pitch between the seven notes that made up the original series (A, B, C, D, E, F, G) *were not all the same*. The difference

Keyboard

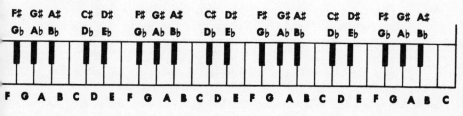

in pitch between A and B, for example, is not the same as the difference between B and C. It takes 440 vibrations per second to produce A, about 500 for B, and about 530 for C. Therefore, B is about 60 vibrations per second faster than A, but C is only about 30 faster than B. This means that it is easy enough to squeeze an A♯ between A and B, giving it about 470 vibrations, and placing it 30 vibrations away from its neighbor on either side; but B and C are already only 30 vibrations apart, so there is no need to insert another tone between them.

95   There are two points in the series where this narrow interval* exists: in addition to the one we have just mentioned (between B and C) there is a similar one between E and F. Therefore, black keys are not needed at those two points, though they are at all the others. That is why the piano keyboard has the white spaces between the groups of black keys.

96   Wherever you see a cluster of *three* black keys, you can be sure immediately that the first one is F♯ (or G♭, to use its other name), the second is G♯ (A♭), and the third is A♯ (B♭). Wherever you see a group of *two* black keys, you can be sure that the first is C♯ (D♭) and the second D♯ (E♭). This makes it easy to spot them at a glance.

97   Theoretically, one can write the note B♯, in addition to those just mentioned, but really it is the same as C on the

*The word **"interval"** is used for the distance in pitch between two tones. The narrow kind of interval described here is called a **"half-step"**; the wider kind a **"whole-step."** (Be sure not to confuse these terms with half-*note* and whole-*note*, which refer to lengths of tones in the rhythmic system.)

piano, because if you raise B enough to sharp it, you will cover the narrow distance to C. In the same way, C♭ can be written, but it really is the same note as plain B. And of course the same holds true for the other narrow point, between E and F: E♯ really sounds the same as F on the piano, and F♭ the same as plain E.*

98   With a little practice, you will be able to spot the right piano key for any note almost automatically, but at first you will find it easier to observe a few visual characteristics by which your eye can distinguish some from others. For instance, if you are looking for a C, observe that it is always the white key just in front of a group of two black ones.

---

*Once in a while you will come across the **"double sharp"** (symbol ✕) and the **"double flat"** (symbol ♭♭). The double sharp raises a tone *two* half-steps, i.e., an additional half-step higher than an ordinary sharp does. The double flat lowers a tone *two* half-steps, i.e., an additional half-step lower than an ordinary flat does. This means that, on the piano, a ✕ or ♭♭ will sound the same as some other note: Consider F ✕ , for instance:

An ordinary F-sharp takes you half the way up to G; therefore, F-*double*-sharp will take you the other half of the way, and will sound the same as G. By the same token, B♭♭ will sound the same as A, for an ordinary B♭ takes us half the way down from B to A, and the ♭♭ will take us the other half of the way. At first glance, this may seem like academic foolishness, but there are some uses of these notes which are explained in the study of harmony; for the present, it is not necessary for you to spend any more time on them.

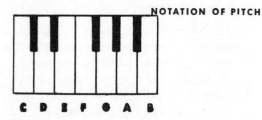

C D E F G A B

If you are looking for an F, it is always the white key in front of *three* black ones. G is always the white key just after the group of three blacks begins (or between the first two blacks in the group of three).

Table of Visual Patterns to Aid in Identifying Notes at the Keyboard

Note	Color of Key	Location	Diagram
C	White	in front of 2 blacks	
D	White	between 2 blacks	
E	White	after 2 blacks	
F	White	in front of 3 blacks	
G	White	between first 2 blacks in a group of 3	

A	White	between last 2 blacks in a group of 3
B	White	after 3 blacks
C♯ (D♭)	Black	1st black in group of 2
D♯ (E♭)	Black	2nd black in group of 2
F♯ (G♭)	Black	1st black in group of 3
G♯ (A♭)	Black	2nd black in group of 3
A♯ (B♭)	Black	3rd black in group of 3
E♯	White	Same as F on piano
F♭	White	Same as E on piano
B♯	White	Same as C on piano
C♭	White	Same as B on piano

99   The C which is written on the piece of line between the two staves (see page 70)

is called **Middle C**, for obvious reasons. It makes a good reference point since it is in the middle of the notation system and approximately in the middle of the piano keyboard. To find it on your piano keyboard, look for the lock or the maker's label, which is at the middle of the keyboard — every piano has one or the other, and some pianos have both. Since we know that the "look" of any C is "a white key just in front of two blacks," we have only to find the example of that pattern which is nearest to the lock or label (usually a little to the left of it), and we'll have not just any C but Middle C. In other words, Middle C is the C which is closest to the center of the piano, but a quick way to find it the first time is to remember that the lock or label is approximately at the center, too. Afterwards, you won't need this artificial aid.

If you see a note written   ,

therefore, you know that it is Middle C and you also know which key to play on the piano in order to produce it. Observe that this same note can also be written another way, using the bass clef and writing the middle note *above* the bass staff,

instead of *below* the treble one:

EXERCISES: THE KEYBOARD

100 Keeping the diagram of the piano keyboard (page 76) before us at first for reference, let's try to locate a few notes at the piano:

Counting up from the line which is G (the clef shows us that, remember), we find that our given note is C.

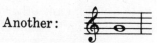

But which C? It is the C above Middle C; an octave above Middle C, to be exact. Therefore, having located Middle C, we have only to look for the C-pattern (white key in front of two blacks) next above it, that is, to the right of it on the keyboard, and we have the one we are seeking.

Another: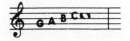

101 This we know immediately to be a G, for it is on the line of the clef itself. But which G? It is the G above Middle C. Now to find any G, as we know, we have to locate a cluster of three blacks, and the G will be the white between the first two blacks. Therefore, look for the cluster of three blacks which is just above Middle C, and then find the G as the white between the first two of them. Let's check our result by another method: having located Middle C, you simply count up through the alphabet on the white keys: C-D-E-F-G, until you come to the white key representing G. It should be the same one we reached a moment ago.

102   Another: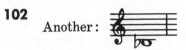

Either by counting down from the clef-note of G, or by
noticing that the given note occupies the space immediately
below Middle C, we find that it is a B with a flat in front
of it. In other words, we have to find on the piano the B-flat
just below Middle C. As the keyboard diagram and the table
show us, B-flat is always the third in each group of three
black keys. Therefore we have only to look for the example
of this pattern just below our Middle C. To check it, we can
count down: the white note in front of C will be B, and the
black note in front of that will be the same B-flat we have
just found.

103   Let's try one more:

Counting up from the clef-line of G (or from any other note
of which we are sure), we find that we have an F with a sharp

in front of it.

The F♯-pattern is "the first black note in a cluster of three."
But this F-sharp is not the one immediately above Middle C.
The F♯ above Middle C is the one which is in the space just
below the clef-line, and looks like this:

Ours, therefore, is an octave higher, so we must find not the first F♯-pattern above Middle C, but the next one after that.

104 Here are some more to practice on your own.* In the bass clef, use the same methods, but remember that this clef points out an F, not a G, and that Middle C is *above* the bass clef, although it is *below* the treble clef.

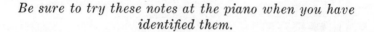

Be sure to try these notes at the piano when you have identified them.

*The letter-names of these notes are given on page 169, but don't look at them until you have solved each case for yourself.

THE KEY SIGNATURE

105   When a composer knows that he is going to use the sharp
or flat form of a certain note frequently throughout a piece
of music, he often writes that sharp or flat at the beginning
of the piece as a warning to the reader. For instance, let's
assume that a composer knows that he is going to use the
flat form of B and the flat form of E often throughout his
composition. He might then write at the beginning of the
piece a flat on the B-line and one on the E-line

as though to say, "Every time you come to B or E in this
piece, play it flat, without any further instruction." This is
a useful shorthand device, as you can see, since one sharp
or flat at the beginning is understood to hold for the whole
composition, unless it is contradicted later. The group of
flats or sharps at the beginning of a piece is called its **key
signature.** (Compare metric signature, page 31.)

106   If the composer wants to contradict a key signature that
he has established, he uses a sign called the **natural** (♮),
which cancels out the flat or sharp that was added. For
example, in the following fragment of a melody the composer uses three flats in his key signature, B-flat, E-flat, and
A-flat, thereby indicating that the reader is to play the flat
forms of B, E, and A, whenever he comes to one of those
three letter-names.

If he should want the As and Bs in the third and fourth
measures not to be flatted, he would have to counteract the

original instructions of his key signature by writing a natural sign in front of those particular notes:

(B♭) (A♭)   (A♮)(B♮)

N.B.: You may have noticed that the stems of some notes are drawn down from their heads, and others up. The purpose of this is to keep the stems from protruding too far above or below the staff where they would get in the way of other staves. The rules are: notes above the middle line are stemmed down, with stem to

left of head {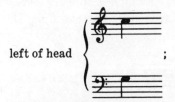} ;

notes below the middle line are stemmed up, with stems to right

of head {} ;

notes on the middle line may be stemmed either way

 ;

hooks are always to the right

107 The conventional practice in music is to consider any change of accidental to hold until the next bar line. For instance, in the case just above, the key signature tells us that B, E, and A are to be flatted whenever they occur in the melody. In order to produce A-natural and B-natural in measure 3, we have to write in the naturals, *which then are assumed to hold for only that measure,* so that they must be written again in measure 4, if we want them there. Since we wrote no accidentals at all in measure 5, it is assumed that the B and A are flatted again in that measure, since the naturals hold only for the measure in which they appear, after which the force of the original key signature is again in effect.

However, an accidental (including a natural) does hold good throughout *all* of the measure in which it appears, even though it cannot go beyond that measure. For example, if measure 4 had read

not only the first A and B would be natural, but the next two also, since they occur in the same measure. If we want the first two eighth-notes natural and the next two flat, we must write in the desired flats:

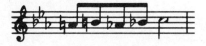

Otherwise the force of the naturals would continue throughout the measure.

108 One other custom or convention with regard to accidentals should be noted. A sharp or flat in the key signature alters all octaves of its letter-name which may occur in the piece, but an accidental in the course of a piece refers only to the

line or space on which it is placed. For example, the F♯ in
this key signature

means that both the high and the low Fs are sharped in
measure 1, but the natural in measure 2 cancels only the top
one, leaving the bottom one still sharp. In other words, a
key signature is general in its application, but an accidental
in the course of a piece is local and specific.

PART THREE

Combination of Rhythmic

and Pitch Notations

Now we are ready to find some simple tunes at the piano from the printed notes.

"AU CLAIR DE LA LUNE"

109

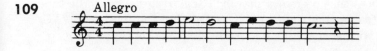
Allegro

First, let's determine the pitches. The first note, as you can discover by counting up from the clef-line of G, is a C, the C above Middle C (which we have already located, on page 83). So we have taken care of the first three notes, since they are all of the same pitch. Once we have this starting point, it really isn't necessary to compute each note separately. The last note in measure 1, for instance, since it is exactly one note above the C, without any sharp or flat, must be D, and the two notes in the next measure must be E and D. As you can see, we often can find the name of a note by comparing it with the notes in front of it, instead of going back to the clef-line all the time. This speeds up the process tremendously.

110 Let's label what we already know in the first two measures and, before we go any further, work out those two completely, just for the satisfaction of doing it. We have:

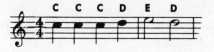

C   C   C   D   E   D

We still don't have the rhythm, but even so, before adding that element, try the sounds of these six notes on the piano, slowly. Find the C above Middle C; now play three of these Cs, then the D to its right, then the E to *its* right, and finally back one step to the same D again. Repeat it slowly:

C-C-C-D-E-D.

111   Now look at the meter and rhythm. The meter is $\frac{4}{4}$, and the tempo is *Allegro* or Fast. Therefore, since there will be four fast beats in each of the two measures, tap steadily with your toe, "**ONE**-two-three-four, **ONE**-two-three-four," at about the speed of a march. The first measure of the tune has four quarter-notes; this means that the four notes C-C-C-D will be spaced one to each beat that we tap: Try it:

And the second measure has two half-notes; so that the E and the D each sounds for two beats or taps, like this:

Now try both measures together, without any pause, tapping steadily with your foot to keep time, and playing the notes C-C-C-D, E–D–, with your right hand. It is a good idea, at this stage, to sing the melody along with the piano as you play it, singing the letter-names of the notes as they go by: "C-C-C-D, E– D–." Remember that the E and D in the second measure are held twice as long as the quarter-notes in the first measure.

112 Look at the next two measures. They involve only notes that we already have learned in the first two measures, so the reading can progress very quickly and easily. By comparing with the first two measures, we see that our new combination is C-E-D-D. C.

Without worrying about the rhythm for the moment, pick out the new notes slowly at the piano: C-E-D-D, C. To do this, you start again with the C above Middle C, then *jump over* one white key to reach E, then back one step to the left for D, then another D, and back to C where we started. Repeat these five notes slowly: C-E-D-D, C.

113 Now the meter and rhythm. Measure 3 has four even quarter-notes, like measure 1, so the four notes C-E-D-D will be spaced one to each beat that we tap. Try that much:

The last measure has just one long C, held for three beats, and a rest on the fourth beat. You must stop in time so that the C does not sound during the fourth beat.

Now do both measures together, without pause, tapping

steadily with your foot, and playing the notes C-E-D-D, C—— with your right hand.

Try it several times, and after the first try, sing along with the melody you are playing. Don't use the words of the song, even if you happen to know them, but use the letter-names so that you learn with which notes they go.

114 Do the whole melody in the same way:

Go over it several times until it feels completely comfortable and "makes sense" to you as you do each note.

Then practice it several times another way: singing *Ta* with each note instead of the letter-names.

115 *If you are patient, you'll find that after a few tries the "look" of a printed note is enough to tell you what it means, without the need for all the computing and figuring we have been doing. After a while, when you have had a little experience, the open white look of the half-note immediately, and without your even thinking about it, will mean to you a sound twice as long as the quarter-note, with its solid black look. And the notes on the staff, going up or down the lines and spaces according to the melody, will relate to each other, and to the sounds with which they belong, in a split second,* *instead of requiring counting from the clef-line or some other key point.*

But be honest with yourself. Don't go on to the second exercise until you are at ease with the first one.

116 When you feel ready, you can try the next melody, which is in ¾ time, and which has a key signature.

"AMERICA"

The key signature warns us in advance that all Fs will be sharped. (If you count up, you will find that the sharp is on the F-line.)

117 Consider only the first two measures, to begin with. The first note is G, the G above Middle C, since it is on the line of the G clef. Therefore, the second note is G, too, and the last one in the measure, which is one step higher than the others, is A.

In the second measure, the first note is in the space just below the G-line, so it must be an F♯ — not just F, but F♯ because the key signature tells us that for this melody all Fs are to be played as F♯s. The next note is G again, and the last one in that measure is A. Even if we had not just determined them in the preceding measure, we could see them at a glance since they move up "by step" from the first note in the measure without skipping any lines or spaces. So far, then, we have:

118   To find these on the piano is a simple task. The first note
is the G above Middle C (white key between the first two
blacks in a group of three blacks), the next is the same, the
A is the next white key to the right. The F♯ in the second
measure is the black key just to the left of the G on which
we began (i.e., the first black in the group of three), then we
have a G and an A which we already know — the two whites
to the right of the F♯. Notice that only three different keys
are used for all the notes in these two measures:

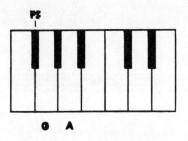

Try these notes, without worrying about the rhythm, and
slowly. G-G-A, F♯-G-A. Do it a few times.

119   Now to add the rhythm. You should already have worked
this one (p. 52), but let's go through it together in detail.
Its familiarity and simplicity will make it all the better as
an illustration of the method.

The metric signature tells us that there are three beats or
pulses in each measure, and the word *"Moderato"* says that
the beats are to go by at a medium speed. Tap with your
foot "ONE-two-three, ONE-two-three," emphasizing the first
beat in each measure, as you have done before. Be sure to
remember that the speed of these beats is slower than those
we have been doing in *"Allegro";* keep the pace slow enough
so that it sounds solemn, and always steady and even.

The first measure of the music has three simple quarter-notes for the G-G-A, so we have only to sound these three tones one to a beat.

Play:

Tap:

But the second measure has a dotted quarter followed by an eighth:

This means that the first note really is held for a quarter plus an eighth — 1½ beats — after which the second note gets only half a beat, and the third note gets exactly one full beat again. In other words, as you tap steadily and evenly

ONE two three

the first note will sound not only for all of "ONE," but also for half of "two." Then the eighth-note will get the remaining half of the "two," and the final quarter-note will come out on "three."

Ta——ta Ta

ONE two three

If you have any trouble with it, mentally subdivide each beat into two halves by thinking "**ONE**-*and*-two-*and*-three-*and*." The taps must be kept exactly the same as before.

ONE *and* two *and* three *and*

Observe that the rhythm of our second measure requires notes on **ONE,** on the *"and"* after "two," and directly on "three."

Start on **ONE,** hold the first note lightly during *"and*-two," sound out again on the *"and"* after "two," and then catch the "three" immediately after it:

120   Now try this rhythm with the correct tones on the piano: F♯-G-A. And combine it with the first measure, which had three even beats on G-G-A. You now have G-G-A, F♯—G-A, with the following relationship of notes and taps:

Play it at the piano slowly, tapping with your foot, and — after the first couple of tries — singing along with the piano. (Sing *Ta* for each note. It would be good practice to sing the letter-names of the notes, but it is rather awkward to squeeze the two syllables of names like "F-sharp" into the sound of a single note.)

121   Let's add the next two measures.

We see immediately that the melody continues by going up still another step after the A which ended measure 2. Moreover, it continues to move by step-wise motion, so it will be easy in general to name each note just by comparing it with the note in front of it, without having to count from the clef-line or any other point. Thus, the first two notes in measure 3 are one step higher than A; they are Bs. And the last note in the measure must be C. In measure 4, the first note is B again, after which the melody goes down through A to G. The tones of measures 3 and 4, then, are B-B-C, B-A-G. Find them on the keyboard and try them several times, without concerning yourself about the rhythm. (If you have any difficulty locating the first B, remember that B is the first white key after a group of three blacks; or count to the right from G.)

122 Now we must add the correct rhythmic values. Here we can find a short cut, if we keep our eyes and ears open, for we can notice that the rhythm of measures 3 and 4 exactly imitates that of measures 1 and 2. That is, measure 3, like measure 1, is made up of three even quarter-notes; and measure 4 has the same dotted rhythm which we have just analyzed in measure 2. *(This sort of thing happens very often in music, and an alert reader can save himself a lot of work by looking for such parallelisms and imitations. They occur most frequently in groups of two measures, as in the case we have been studying, or in groups of four measures.)* So all you have to do is play the new notes to the same rhythm that was used for the first two measures.

123 Put the four measures together:

124 Finally, the last two measures, which are relatively easy:

The notes are A-G-F♯, G, all of which we have worked out in the earlier measures of the melody. Try them a couple of times. The rhythm of measure 5 is simply three even quarter-notes, and measure 6 contains just one long note (a dotted half-note) which fills all three beats of the measure.

125 Now to put all six measures of "America" together. Tap a steady pulse, emphasizing the **ONE** of each measure slightly, and sing *Ta* for each printed note as you play it.

126 Not all melodies begin on the first beat of the measure.
Some of them take a kind of "running start" of one or more
light beats before landing on the first beat. This preparatory
fraction of a measure is called an **upbeat.** In the following
example,

THE DOXOLOGY ("Old Hundred")

Praise God from Whom all bless- ings flow,

the first printed note is an upbeat, and it receives less
emphasis than the second note, which falls on the downbeat,
the strong beat of the measure. Understand that one beat is
not faster or slower than another. It is not a question of
speed, for all the metric beats, including the upbeat and
downbeat, must go at the same speed to preserve the steady
pulse on which the whole system of meter is based. But the
downbeat gets a little more weight or stress than the upbeat.
The feel of the upbeat is one of preparation, as though one
took a deep breath or lifted himself on his toes before walking off into the downbeat of the melody.

Later we will learn the symbols used to mark a note which
is to receive a sharp accent or emphasis, but even an ordinary
bar line means that the beat which follows it, since it is the
first beat of a measure, will be somewhat heavier than the
other beats. Theoretically, this bar line accent should exist
only in the mind of the reader, for the sake of grouping the

beats into measures, but in actual practice it often coincides with a real accent, in which a note is sung or played with extra force to make it stand out.

127   While we are at it, let's do the whole of the "Doxology," since it gives us a chance to try another key signature, and to learn a useful new symbol.

The rhythmic pattern is extremely easy — every note in the melody is a quarter-note!* But at four points (every

*There is another version of this tune, which some readers may know, in which the rhythm is slightly different, although the tones are the same in pitch. (See the footnote on page 53.) In the second version some notes are twice as long as others, instead of all being quarter-notes. It goes like this:

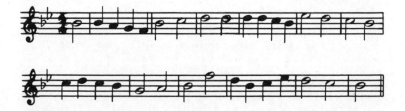

Even the upbeat on the first word takes twice as long as in the first version. If you know this hymn the second way, it will be interesting for you to compare the rhythms. *First* study carefully the analysis given in Sections 127 through 135, as though you had never heard the melody before, and then try to determine the differences indicated by the other notation.

second measure) the following new symbol appears over a note:

⌒ . It is called a **hold** or **fermata** (or sometimes, from its appearance, a "corona" or a "bird's-eye") and it tells the musician that the regular counting of beats is to be stopped for a moment while the note under the fermata is held. It is only a temporary interruption of the steady flow of the beats in the measure, and, after the holding of the indicated note, the music resumes its regular pulse again. In hymn tunes like this one, the fermata usually marks the end of a line of the words.

128 There is no rule about how long a fermata should be held. In theory, it means only that the regular counting is temporarily suspended, and therefore a note marked with a fermata might be *shorter* than its normal value instead of longer. In other words, it indicates merely that a slight liberty is being taken with the rhythm, without specifying the exact extent of that liberty. In practice, however, the fermata almost always means that the note so marked is to be "stretched" beyond its written value, and most musicians will hold it to perhaps twice the written length. In the last analysis, the performer's decision as to the length of a fermata will vary with his taste, his metabolism, the musical context, and a dozen other relevant and irrelevant factors. The fermata, like the tempo indication *(Allegro, Andante,* etc.), is an approximating instruction, not a determining one, and some contemporary composers tend to avoid it because of its inexactness. But it is present in much music, both old and new, precisely in those places where exactness is not desired, and the student must learn its use in our system of notation.

129 The effect of the fermatas in the tune we have been considering is to make us "sit" a little longer on the last word of each line of the poem (i.e., on the third beat of every second measure), after which the music continues in strict time again, with the beat after the fermata acting as an upbeat to the next measure.

130 You will notice that when a piece begins with an upbeat, an equivalent beat is often subtracted from the final measure, as though to compensate for the fact that the piece began a beat before the first full measure. Thus, the first and the final measures, each incomplete in itself, add up to one full measure.

131 Notice, too, that when a piece continues for several lines, it is customary to write the clef and the key signature (sharps or flats) on each line, but the metric signature only at the beginning of the first line.

132 Now we must work out the details of this tune. The key signature tells us that all Bs and Es are to be read B-flat and E-flat respectively. The first note is on the B-line (as you can verify, if necessary, by counting up from the clef-line), so it will be the B-flat above Middle C. The next four notes, moving down step by step, must be B-flat, A, G, F, therefore. The second measure begins again on B-flat, and moves up step by step to C and D. Let's take this much separately, since the fermata on the D indicates that it is the

end of the phrase. We now have B♭| B♭-A-G-F| B♭-C-D̂
beginning on the B♭ above Middle C. The B♭ pattern is "the
third black key in a group of three," so we have only to find
the particular B♭ which is above Middle C. After this we
move down (to the left) through the white note in front
of it (A), to the white notes for G and F. The second measure
begins again on the B♭, but moves up (to the right) through
the white notes for C (be sure you find C, not B-natural)
and D.

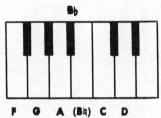

Try this much, slowly tapping the beats, and holding the D,
as its fermata indicates, when you come to it.

133 Take the next phrase. It begins on the same note with
which we just ended, D, and indeed the next two notes are
merely repetitions of the D, followed by C and B♭. The next
measure then jumps to the space above D, i.e., E-flat (remember that the key signature makes all Es flat in this melody),
after which we move down step by step to D and C (with
fermata). Play the notes of the second phrase, beginning on
the D which ended the first phrase, and observing that E-flat

is "the second black key in a group of two blacks," or "the black key immediately to the right of D."

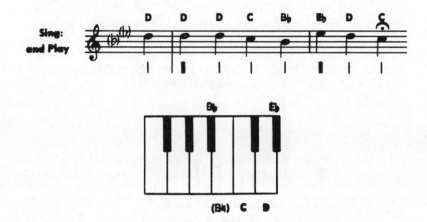

134 After this point you should be able to work out the rest of the tune at the keyboard for yourself. The only new note will be the high F, which is the upbeat to the last phrase, and that will be easy to locate from your charts, especially since its pattern will be the same as that of the low F at the end of the first measure (a white in front of three blacks), but an octave higher. Try the whole melody several times, tapping to keep time, but holding the beat wherever the fermata tells you to do so.

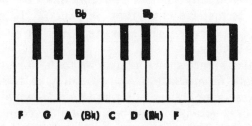

135 In the last phrase, when the melody skips from F down to D and then to Bb, and again from C to Eb, you may have to go over it again and again until you get used to making skips on the keyboard. But you will find that very soon this will be part of your general knowledge along with the simpler stepwise motion.

136 The next example, the familiar chorus of "Jingle Bells," is purposely presented here in the bass clef (F clef) because most of our previous exercises have emphasized the treble clef (G clef) and we should have some experience with both of them.

"JINGLE BELLS"

We have already made a start on this one, at least with
respect to meter and rhythm, on page 52. It is in $\frac{2}{4}$ meter,
Allegro, and the key signature tells us that all Bs are to be
read as B-flats.

A quick glance shows us that we come to rest on our first
long note in measure 4, so we can take these first four
measures as a phrase or unit and study them at one time.

The first note is an A, as we can tell by counting up from
the clef-line: F-G-A. More precisely, it is the *A below Middle
C,* since it is on the top line of the bass staff, and the line
for Middle C comes between the top line of the bass staff and
the bottom line of the treble staff. So the first two measures
consist of nothing but As! The third measure jumps from A
up to C (Middle C, with its piece of line added above the
staff), then down to F (the clef-line), after which it moves
up stepwise through G, to the A which fills measure 4.

Using the chart, if you need it, locate these on the keyboard
and try them a few times.

137 Now to add the rhythm. The metric signature tells us that
there are two beats to each measure. They should go by
briskly because they are marked *Allegro,* but at first let's
take them a bit more slowly than we know they should be,
just to make it easier; when we have worked out the whole
thing, we can try it at a faster speed. I suggest that you take
the two beats considerably slower at first than you would
the "LEFT-right" of a march.

The first measure has two eighth-notes on the first beat
and a quarter-note on the second beat. This means that if
you sing it with the syllable *Ta* on each note, you will have

to sing two *Tas* while you tap **ONE,** and one *Ta* for the second beat, like this:

The second measure is exactly the same. The third measure has four even eighth-notes, so each beat will get two *Tas*:

And the fourth measure has just one long note, a half-note, over the two beats of the measure:

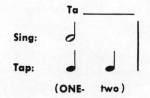

Altogether, the four measures go this way in rhythm:

Combining this with the pitch notation, you now have:

138   The next four measures have more variety in notation — mostly in the rhythm, for the pitch relationships are very simple:

Measure 5 has only one pitch in it, B-flat. Measure 6 has one B-flat, followed by four As. Measure 7 has A-G-G-A; and measure 8 has G-C. Locate these on the keyboard — Bb-Bb-Bb-Bb, Bb-A-A-A-A, A-G-G-A, G-C — even before you do the rhythm, so that you have a general idea of the outline of the melody.

139   As for the rhythms, we have already worked out every one of these patterns on pages 36, 37, and 52. Review them if necessary. Notice that the sixteenth-note at the end of measure 5 comes after the *"and"* of "two" (when you count **ONE**-*and*-two-*and*); or you can think of that sixteenth-note as one quick upbeat to the next measure, almost as though measure 5 were essentially this rhythm

(instead of   )

with the one short sixteenth-note stolen from the end of the quarter-note to make an upbeat over the bar to measure 6. Notice that the rhythm of measure 6 is almost the same as this simple rhythm:

,

the only difference being that the last eighth-note is divided into two sixteenths. Measure 7 is, of course, precisely the rhythm of four equal eighth-notes, and measure 8 of two even quarters.

140 Try those four measures in our established way, tapping steadily two beats to each measure, and singing on the syllable *Ta* as you play the notes on the piano. If you stumble at any point, analyze the way in which that place is put together, and then try the whole thing a little more slowly. You can increase the speed later, when you have licked the problem. *DON'T* keep repeating a passage that gives you trouble if you are going to make the same mistake each time. Figure it out calmly and then try it again. Why? Because you learn by practice and repetition, and if you repeat a wrong thing often enough, you will learn the wrong thing just as thoroughly and efficiently by practicing it as you would the right one.

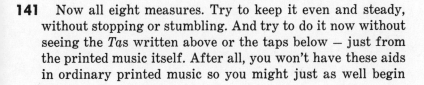

141 Now all eight measures. Try to keep it even and steady, without stopping or stumbling. And try to do it now without seeing the *Ta*s written above or the taps below — just from the printed music itself. After all, you won't have these aids in ordinary printed music so you might just as well begin

weaning yourself away from them, now that they have
served their purpose.

142 Once again we can save ourselves a good bit of work by
keeping on the alert. We can observe that the second half of
"Jingle Bells," measures 9 to 16, is very similar to the first
half. (Compare page 107.) In fact, the first six measures of
each half are exactly the same! It is only the last two measures which are different. Therefore, if we repeat in measures
9 to 14 what we have already worked out for measures 1 to
6, only 15 and 16 will remain to be done. You should do this
for yourself, reading all sixteen measures in order when you
have finished, trying not to stumble, hesitate, or alter the
tempo. Do it slowly at first so that you can keep it even,
without straining at the difficult spots; and increase the
speed only when you can do the whole melody faster, not
only the easy parts. Be especially careful to keep the beat
steady in measures 5 and 6, which have a little more rhythmic variety than the rest.

PART FOUR

Supplementary Symbols and Devices

143 The notation system includes a number of auxiliary symbols and devices which are not basic parts of it, like the rhythm and pitch indications, but are necessary to supplement them. Most of them are shorthand devices, designed to make the job of writing music a little less laborious. You must already have discovered that it is a slow and tedious business to put music down on paper, and musicians are always seeking short cuts and abbreviations.

REPETITIONS

144 For instance, since the second half of "Jingle Bells" (page 107) duplicates much of the first half, it obviously would save time and work if the repetition of the six measures (9 to 14) could be shown by a symbol, instead of being written out. This can be done as follows:

At the end of measure 8 you will observe a double bar with

two dots in front of it, like this ‖ . This is a **repeat**

sign. It instructs you to go back to the beginning and play or sing the whole thing over again exactly as you did the first time. If the composer doesn't want to go all the way back to the beginning, he puts a similar sign, but **facing**

the other way   ‖:   at the point where you should begin

your repeat. Just to illustrate, let's pretend that he wants
you to repeat only the last four measures of the tune; then
he would use the repeat signs in this way:

You would then repeat only the four measures between the
dots.

145   You must also have noticed that measures 7 and 8 have
this sign over them ⌈1.   ⌉ and that they are followed
by two more measures marked thus: ⌈2.   ⌉

This instructs the reader that he is to play or sing the
measures marked   ⌈1.   ⌉

the first time through, but that in making the repeat, he
is to substitute for them the measures marked

Measures 7 and 8 are called the **first ending,** and the other two measures the **second ending.** Their use saves the copying of six measures in this case, and of whole pages in some compositions.

146 Sometimes, especially in long pieces, the composer will indicate a repeat by writing **D.C.,** which is an abbreviation for the Italian words *da capo,* meaning "from the head" or "from the top." If he wants you to go back to some special point, but not all the way to the beginning, he may mark

that special point with a sign, either ⊕ or ✗ , and write

D.S. which is an abbreviation for the Italian words *dal segno,* meaning "from the sign."

147 If the phrase **al fine** ("to the end") is added **(D.C. al fine, or D.S. al fine),** it means that you are to go back to the beginning or to the sign, as the case may be, but repeat only until you reach the word *Fine* ("end") written in the music. Here are two examples each of which includes an ordinary repeat sign as well as a **D.C.** or **D.S.**:

"THE MARINE'S HYMN"*

*Sometimes you may hear this tune in a slightly different version, with the following tones in measures 5 and 6:

"OLD FOLKS AT HOME"

148 Notice that in "The Marine's Hymn" the repeat instructions occur after only part of the measure has gone by (i.e., there are only three beats, instead of the four which we expect in $\frac{4}{4}$ meter, in the last printed measure where the *D.C.* appears). A *Da Capo*, a *Dal Segno*, or an ordinary repeat sign, need not come at the end of a measure; it may be used anywhere within the measure. This is especially frequent in pieces which begin with an upbeat, as "The Marine's Hymn" does.

149 When the composer wants one whole measure to be repeated, he saves himself the trouble of writing it a second time by using this sign between the bar lines of the second measure:

$$| \mathcal{Z} |$$

For example, the first four measures of "Jingle Bells" could be written this way:

If a composer, for any reason, wants to repeat a measure several times, he may use as many of these signs as he finds necessary:

150 When single notes must be repeated, as they often must, especially in instrumental music, there are still other shorthand devices. A beam, over or under a single note, is understood to divide the note into the shorter values indicated by the beam: for instance, a half-note with an eighth-note beam through · its stem, means "a half-note's worth of eighth-notes":

A whole-note with a double beam under or over it means "a whole-note's worth of sixteenth-notes" (sixteenths because of the *double* beam):

Here are a number of additional examples:

151   The word **tremolo** (abbreviated **trem.**) written over one of these beamed notes means that the note is to be repeated as fast as possible, without sticking literally to the number of subdivisions indicated by the beams. Thus,

does not mean that the half-note is to be divided into exact thirty-second-notes or sixty-fourth-notes, but that the player is to repeat Bs as fast as he possibly can.

152   Often it is desired to repeat, not a single tone, but a pair
of alternating tones, like this:

This can be abbreviated by writing both of the notes involved
as half-notes (in this case) but adding the double beam for
sixteenth-notes to connect their stems:

It is as though we said, "A half-note's worth of alternating
Es and Cs in sixteenths." Notice the difference between this
abbreviation and the one for repeated notes without alternation:

but

It is the beam *connecting* the two half-notes which calls for
alternation instead of simple repetition.   This symbol cannot be confused with a pair of ordinary sixteenth-notes
because of the hollow white heads of the half-notes; ordinary
sixteenth-notes would have solid black heads, of course:

ORNAMENTS

153   The symbol **tr** indicates a **trill,** which is a rapid alternation of the given note with the note just above it. For example, if you see the *tr* over the note B, you play a rapid alternation of Bs and Cs:

Notice that we have said "approximately," for the trill does not require any specific number of alternations, or any specific speed of alternation. In general, one alternates the two notes involved as rapidly as possible, until the written value of the given note is used up. You will notice that this is very much like the principle of the tremolo. Thus, in the instance cited here, one would not have exactly eight thirty-second-notes, but rather "a quarter-note's worth of Bs and Cs, alternating as fast as possible." The effect is to embellish or decorate the B.

It is also permissible to begin with the embellishing note (the upper one). That is,

beginning the trill on the C instead of the B. Many performers use this second interpretation of the trill in seventeenth- and eighteenth-century music; the first type, with the given note at the beginning, is more common in nineteenth- and twentieth-century music.

154   The trill is only one of a great many so-called **ornaments** used in music. They are very seldom encountered in the music of our time, but they were extremely common in the music of the seventeenth and eighteenth centuries. The study of the old ornamentation is a forbiddingly complex one. Not only the scholars of today, but even the authorities of the seventeenth and eighteenth centuries, disagree constantly on the way in which some of the symbols are to be read and interpreted. Therefore, it is impossible to make general and simple rules, and unless one has really studied the whole literature of these centuries and knows the context in which each example occurs, it is fruitless to become involved in the perpetual arguments about them.

At the risk of oversimplifying the problem, we will nevertheless give here one rule of thumb which covers the most common kind of ornament, the **grace-note,** since the student is likely to encounter it even in relatively simple music. The grace-note, printed usually as a miniature eighth-note, with a little crossbar through the stem and hook, ♪ is used for notes so short that it is not necessary to bother with computing their exact length. The grace-note is not counted at all in adding up the beats in a measure, and its time usually is stolen from one of the more important notes on either side of it (most often from the preceding one, but sometimes from the following one). For example,

There is another kind of grace-note, which is printed *without* the little crossbar through the stem, as a miniature sixteenth-note, eighth-note, or even quarter-note. It is found in old music:

Written:

*The first way is more common; the second is more correct.

This grace-note without the crossbar seems generally to have been played as though it were a real note of the value indicated by its stem and hooks (its value being taken out of the following note, to which it was tied) :

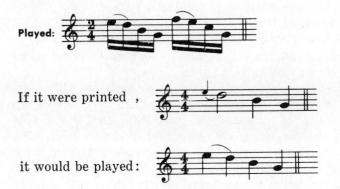

Played:

If it were printed ,

it would be played:

If you ask why such an illogical custom was adopted, and why these passages were not written in the first place as they were meant to sound, the answer is that they arose at a time when strict rules of musical composition limited the tones which properly could appear on a strong beat, and any others had to be shown or explained in their relationship to these permitted ones.

SYMBOLS FOR DYNAMICS

155   Acquaintance with a few more abbreviations and symbols, related neither to rhythm nor pitch, but to **dynamic level** (how loud or soft the sounds are to be), is necessary for reading music.

These symbols are usually printed just below the music staff.

156   The Italian word *forte,* meaning loud or strong, is abbreviated to the letter *f*. *Piano,* meaning soft, is abbreviated to *p*.

From these two, a whole series of gradations is evolved. *Fortissimo* ("very loud") is abbreviated *ff* . *Pianissimo* ("very soft") is *pp* . Between *f* and *p*, there are *mezzo forte* (medium loud, a little softer than *forte)*, abbreviated *mf* , and *mezzo piano* (medium soft, a little louder than *piano)*, abbreviated *mp*. Occasionally it is useful to represent a degree of loudness even greater than *ff* ; in such cases, *fff* is used. Similarly for something even softer than *pp*, we write *ppp* .

157 The symbol *fp* *(fortepiano)* indicates that the tone so marked is to be begun *forte* but immediately dropped to *piano*. *Sforzato* and *sforzando* (abbreviated *sf* , *sfz* , or *fz* , meaning "forced" or "forcing"), are slightly different — tones so marked are to be suddenly forced or accented, but there is no indication that they are to be dropped to *piano* immediately afterward.

158 If the music is to grow gradually louder, instead of suddenly, the word *crescendo* ("growing") appears. It is abbreviated *cresc*. *Diminuendo* and *decrescendo*, abbreviated *dim*. and *decresc*., respectively, show that the music is to grow gradually softer. Sometimes *crescendo* is indicated, without any words, by the symbol

and *decrescendo* or *diminuendo* by the symbol

159 For more of these terms, consult Appendix Two (See p. 155).

If a composer wants you to give a special accent or emphasis to a note, beyond that which it would normally receive, he can put the **accent mark** over that note. It looks like this:

$>$. For example:

Some musicians write the accent mark vertically, instead of horizontally, like this:

SYMBOLS FOR ARTICULATION, STYLE, ETC.

160   **Dots** over or under notes indicate that they are to be played in a short, crisp fashion, each note separated from the surrounding notes. This is called *staccato,* from the Italian word meaning "separated." In effect, this really means that they are played a little shorter than they are written:

at a fast or moderate tempo is aproximately the same as

161   If pointed **wedges** are used instead of dots, they are taken to indicate an even more crisply separated execution, that is, more staccato:

is played approximately

In addition, the wedge often adds a sort of hammered, almost accented quality to a note.

162   The opposite of staccato, that is, the smooth connection of notes, is indicated by the **slur**:

Notes so marked are to be played or sung as smoothly as possible, without any interruption between them. This style is called *legato,* from the Italian word meaning "bound together." Notice that this is really the same symbol that is used for the tie. (See p. 15). It is called a tie when it connects notes of the *same* pitch so that they become one longer note, whereas it is called a slur when it connects notes of *different* pitch so that they are played or sung smoothly and without individual articulation. Really the tie is just a special case of the slur — the case where two notes are connected so smoothly that they become one note. It is even possible to have a tie under a slur, when a note which has been lengthened by the use of a tie is to be connected smoothly to a different note:

Here the lower of the two curved lines is a tie which is required to make one continuous D by joining the half-note D in the first measure with the quarter-note D in the second measure; the upper curved line is a slur which connects the resultant D smoothly with the B.

163   This is a good time to note that ties and slurs affect the rule about accidentals differently. You will remember that, in general, a flat or sharp is assumed to hold for all of the measure in which it appears (See p. 88 ff.). Since a tie makes one long note of two shorter ones, an accidental before the tied note will hold for the entire length of the tie, even when it carries over into a second measure:

Here the flat applies not only for the second beat of measure 1, but also over the bar for the first beat of measure 2, since these two beats have been united into one by the tie. If there were no tie, it would be assumed that the flat lasted only to the end of the measure, and that the first beat of measure 2 was natural:

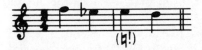

In such cases, some musicians write in an extra natural (although theoretically it is superfluous) just to make sure that the reader understands their meaning:

Often they will put the extra accidental in parentheses, as has been done here, to show that it is not really necessary but is supplied to avoid doubt in the reader's mind.

164   When such a sharped or flatted note is tied over into the next measure, therefore, the accidental holds till the end of the tie, but not for the rest of the second measure. For instance, if another E were to occur in the second measure after the tie, it would be read as E-natural:

since the force of the flat would have expired with the end of the tie. Even a slur over the whole phrase would make no difference, since a slur shows only a smooth style of performance and does not affect the length or pitch of the notes under it.

165 **Dashes** over notes indicate a slight lengthening. Some performers actually make such tones a trifle longer than written, but most interpret the dash or "long mark" to indicate the holding of the separate notes to the full extent of their value, with as little break as possible between notes. This is slightly different from the legato slur, which actually binds notes together into a single smooth phrase. The dashes leave the notes separate, but with as little "air space" as possible between them.

166 Occasionally you will see **dots under a slur,** an apparent contradiction. The intention of this notation is to combine the conspicuous qualities of both dots and slurs — that is, to give the over-all effect of notes that belong together in a phrase, yet to separate them slightly from each other. It is a sort of compromise between the two.

is played approximately like

The breaks between notes are very slight, the player becomes aware that a continuous phrase is desired, and even his awareness helps to communicate this effect to the listener.

167 In *vocal music,* when words are printed with a melody, the notation sometimes is so arranged as to make the separate syllables of the words apparent at a glance. This is done by using **separate hooks** for eighths and sixteenths (or any other notes with hooks), instead of beams, whenever they are to be sung with separate text syllables; beams are saved for the cases where several eighths or sixteenths are sung to one syllable. An example will make this clear. Suppose the words "Never to return" are set to music as follows:

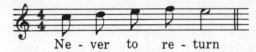

Since each syllable gets a separate tone, separate hooks are used, and the reader knows immediately how the notes fit the syllables. This phrase would *not* be written with a beam in vocal music, although in instrumental music the beam would be considered easier to read, since there would be no question of reading syllables of words:

(The same phrase as written for instrumental music, but not *for vocal music.)*

168 If a single syllable gets two or more eighth- or sixteenth-notes (or any other kind of note that has a hook), a beam is used to show that they are all sung to one syllable. For instance, if the last syllable in the example above were sung to four eighth-notes instead of one half-note,

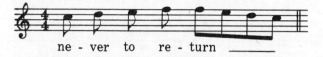

ne - ver to   re - turn _____

a beam would be used for the last four eighths to show that
all of them are sung over a single syllable, "-turn."

169   Strictly speaking, a slur is needed to show that the last
four eighths above are sung *smoothly* to one syllable, but
since the beam is assumed to suggest as much, the slur is
often omitted in such cases. Occasionally, however, the student will see such a passage printed with both beam and slur:

Ne - ver to   re - turn _____

170   The slur is more necessary when the notes sung to one
syllable are of longer value than eighths, because such notes
cannot be grouped under a beam. If "-turn" were sung to
two quarter-notes, a slur would be advisable to indicate the
smooth joining of the two notes during the singing of the
one syllable:

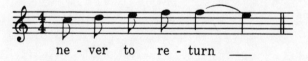

ne - ver to   re - turn ___

171   Note that a hyphen, or a string of hyphens, is used between
syllables of a word, but that a continuous line is used at the
end of a word, or for a word of one syllable, when it is desired
to suggest the flow of music during that word.

172   Here is "Jingle Bells" written as instrumental music (as
we did it before, on p. 113), and then as vocal music with
words. Observe carefully the differences in the use of beams.

Instrumental:

Vocal with words:

Jin- gle bells, Jin - gle bells, Jin - gle all the

way. Oh what fun it is to ride in a

1.
one horse o - pen sleigh. _____

2.
one horse o - pen sleigh.

PART FIVE

Tonality

173 With the information you now have, plus that contained in the Appendices, you should be able to read any simple melody. However, there is an important concept behind most of the melodies you will encounter, the understanding of which will make your reading of music more intelligent and more meaningful — the concept of **tonality.**

174 In almost any melody, one tone can be found which seems more important, more final, than any of the others used in making the melody. Instead of trying to explain this in words, let's illustrate by inventing a laboratory melody with which to experiment. Here is a simple one of four measures, using the tones C-D-E-F-G-A in various combinations:

First you must try it at the piano, singing along on the syllable *Ta* as we have done in the past. Since there are no flats and sharps, we know that the whole melody can be played on the white keys. The first note is Middle C, after which the melody moves up through D, E, and F on the white keys (measure 1). In measure 2, we move back through E and D, and then jump up to A. (Consult your keyboard chart, if you have to.) This is the first phrase, two measures long. In the last two measures, the melody moves down through G, F, and E, returns for one note to F, then continues down again until it reaches the Middle C on which it began. The rhythm should be simple for you, mostly even quarter notes, with a half-note to end each phrase. Try the tune over as many times as necessary, until you are perfectly sure of it, since it is going to serve as our guinea pig in this experiment. It would be a good idea to memorize it if you can:

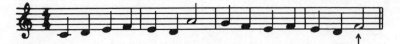

175 Now, if you substitute various other tones for the last C, you will find that none of them sounds as satisfactorily final as the C. For instance, try an F as the last note instead of C:

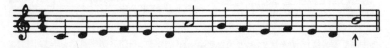

I think you will agree that the melody sounds somehow "incomplete" with the F.

176 Try another tone, B for example:

This sounds even less finished than the F, or at any rate, not so final as the original C. (At this point, you may want to play it again in its original form, just to remind yourself how the C did sound.)

177 Try D:

Better than the B, perhaps, but certainly not so good as the C.

178 Try E and G:

These may seem a little more stable than some of the others, but a comparison with the C will convince you that it remains the most naturally conclusive tone of all.

179 If you experiment with some of the black keys, you will find that they sound even more remote. You might try F♯, D♯, or any others you wish:

180 In other words, for this particular melody, the C seems to be the most satisfactory final note, the note toward which the others insist on gravitating, as though some strong force were pulling them there. The other notes have varying degrees of restfulness or activity, with respect to the C, and if we wished we could arrange them in a sort of table of relative activity.

181 This is true of most melodies — that some single tone usually tends to assert itself as the principal one. This central tone is known as the **tonic** (or sometimes, the **key center**), and a piece of music in which the other tones are related to such a key center is said to be *tonal*. The whole concept of this relationship to a central tone is called **tonality**.

182 When, as in our experimental melody above, the final pull is toward C, the piece is said to be "in the key of C." Each melody has its own tonic or key center. If the tonic is G, the melody is "in the key of G"; if the tonic is E-flat, the melody is "in the key of E-flat," and so on. A melody need not end on its tonic, although it usually does; when it is clear from the nature of the melody which is the tonic, the composer sometimes takes the liberty of ending on one of the closely related tones other than the tonic.

183 The key of E-flat consists of a certain group of notes, all related in varying degrees to their tonic, E-flat; the key of G has another group, all related to G; the key of F♯ has another group, all related to F♯. These groups are called **scales.** When we state the key of a piece of music, we are giving a sort of alphabet or vocabulary of the tones available for use in that piece. They may be arranged in all sorts of different combinations. Tones outside the key occasionally may be introduced in passing, but will never assume the importance of those directly related to the tonic.

184 When we know the name of the tonic, therefore, we know pretty well, after a little experience, which tones to expect in its company. The key of C, for example, will have all "white" notes (naturals), no sharps or flats. The key of E-flat will have several flats and the rest natural. The key of A will have several sharps and the rest natural. In other words, for each key there will be a characteristic key signature.

185 To explain how this works is a bit more complicated. Since it is not absolutely necessary at this stage of the game (after all, you have already been reading melodies provided with key signatures, without knowing how they were related to their keys), the explanation is given in the following Appendix where the ambitious student can find it if he wishes to penetrate further. However, it would be more advisable at this point to find a good instructor for the more advanced study, or at least to consult a good textbook. Paul Hindemith's *Elementary Training for Musicians* (Associated Music Publishers, N. Y.) is highly recommended for the serious student, as well as the early pages of William Mitchell's *Elementary Harmony* (Norton, N. Y.).

Scales and Key Signatures

186 We know that there are only twelve different tones from which all our melodies are made: the white notes on the piano keyboard account for seven of them — A B C D E F G, the black notes for the other five — F♯ G♯ A♯ C♯ D♯. (Of course the five black notes can also be called by their flat names — G♭ A♭ B♭ D♭ E♭ — but they are the same five keys on the piano.)

187 Some melodies use all twelve of these tones in various patterns and combinations, but most melodies use only seven or eight of them. In fact, you can construct perfectly good melodies with fewer elements than that; for instance, you might try using only the five black keys and making up melodies for yourself at the piano keyboard. If you take them in different rhythms, and rearrange the order of the five notes in all possible ways, moving sometimes smoothly from one to the next and jumping around at other times, you will find that there are countless pleasant melodies to be made from these five tones alone. The only limit is the inventiveness of the composer!

"Auld Lang Syne" is a familiar tune which can be played on the black keys alone:

Others are "Swing Low, Sweet Chariot," "Nobody Knows the Trouble I've Seen," and "Short'nin' Bread," to mention just a few.

SCALES

188   If you want to find the group of notes, or scale (see p. 134), from which any melody is built, you have only to a) list all the tones used in the melody, b) eliminate any duplications, and c) arrange in alphabetical order what remains, *beginning with the tonic.*

189   For instance, the "Doxology," which we used in Chapter III (p. 102), has the following notes:

If we eliminate the repetitions of notes which are used more than once, we have: Bb A G F C D Eb. And if we arrange them in alphabetical order, beginning with the tonic (which is Bb, as you can test by trying to end with some other tone), we have: Bb C D Eb F G A. This is the scale on which the "Doxology" is based. In other words, it is the inventory of the raw material from which the melody is made.

THE MAJOR SCALE

190 Theoretically the number of such scales from which melodies can be made is very great, but during the past few hundred years, European and American composers have tended to use only two or three of these scales for most of their music. The most common one is called the **major scale,** and the simplest example of it can be obtained by taking the white keys on the piano, from one C to the C an octave higher: C D E F G A B C. Such a scale has seven different tones, plus the repetition of the tonic at the end, one octave higher — or eight tones in all. The tones which make up a scale are called its *steps* or *degrees*.

191 Now you will remember that the white keys, although they seem on the surface to be equal, really have differing distances or "intervals" between them. The distances in pitch from B to C, and from E to F, are half-steps, whereas the distances between the other notes are whole-steps.* Therefore, the scale from C to C has the following succession of whole-steps and half-steps:

C   D   E   F   G   A   B   C

Whole Whole *Half* Whole Whole Whole *Half*

192 *This is what characterizes a major scale:* that its eight tones, when arranged in alphabetical order, beginning with the tonic, will always have a half-step between the 3rd and 4th tones, a half-step between the 7th and 8th tones, and whole-steps everywhere else:

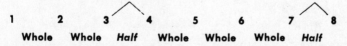

1   2   3   4   5   6   7   8

Whole Whole *Half* Whole Whole Whole *Half*

It is the small interval between the 7th and 8th tones which
*See page 78.

is perhaps the most distinctive feature of the major scale, for the 7th tone, as a result of it, gives the impression of always being drawn strongly toward the near-by eighth tone, which is the tonic. The tonic in the major scale is definitely the center of attraction.

CONSTRUCTING MAJOR SCALES

193 In the scale of white notes from C to C, the half-steps fall in the right places to produce a major scale. But this is not quite so if you begin the white-note series on G:

1	2	3	4	5	6	7	8
G	A	B	C	D	E	F	G
Whole	Whole	*Half*	Whole	Whole	*Half*	Whole	

Here the first half-step occurs between the 3rd and 4th tones, it is true, but the other half-step falls between the 6th and 7th, instead of between the 7th and 8th. Indeed, since there is a whole step between the 7th and 8th in this scale, the major scale's characteristic drive of the 7th step toward the 8th (tonic) will be absent.

194 If it is desired to construct a major scale beginning on G, however, this can be done by analogy with the one on C. It will be necessary to do a little "plastic surgery" on the upper part of the scale to imitate the basic pattern which requires a half-step between 7 and 8 (and a whole-step between 6 and 7). This can be achieved easily by using F♯ instead of F.

1	2	3	4	5	6	7	8
G	A	B	C	D	E	F♯	G
Whole	Whole	*Half*	Whole	Whole	Whole	*Half*	

By raising the F a half-step to make it F♯, we bring it closer to G, so that the F♯ now has the same relationship to its tonic, G, that the B in the model scale had to its tonic, C.

Moreover, by raising the F to F♯, we have killed another bird with the same stone — we have enlarged the space between E and F (6 and 7) from a half-step to the desired whole-step. In other words, with the use of F♯ instead of F, we can make a major scale beginning on G which has the same plan as the major scale beginning on C.

Compare:

1	2	3	∧	4	5	6	7	∧	8
G	A	B		C	D	E	F♯		G

Whole Whole *Half* Whole Whole Whole *Half*

1	2	3	∧	4	5	6	7	∧	8
C	D	E		F	G	A	B		C

195 Throughout any melody using this scale on G, the tendency will be to have all the Fs sharp, and none of them natural, and it will save much writing in of the sharp, if we put it in the key signature at the beginning, once and for all. "America," the first part of which we studied on p. 95, can serve as an example of a piece written "in the key of G major." Here is the entire melody:

If you eliminate the doubles, and write the different notes employed in alphabetical order, beginning on the tonic G, you will have the following array: G A B C D E F♯ (G).

196   Actually the high G does not appear in this melody; it is the *low* F♯ which is drawn toward the *low* G, but the principle is the same, since the 8th tone of a major scale is always a duplication of the name of the first, as you will remember, and is introduced, in the scale, just for the sake of making clearer the gravitational pull of 7 toward the tonic (see page 139). The higher octave sometimes may not be included in the actual melody or, on the other hand, additional octaves, still higher, may be included without affecting the fundamental nature of the relationship: a tonic is a tonic, and it will act as a tonal magnet, drawing the 7th degree of the scale toward it, whether they are in the middle of the keyboard, way up at the high end, or down at the low end, whether they are sung by a voice, or played on an instrument.

197   A major scale can be constructed, beginning on any of the twelve tones, white or black, just as we constructed one on G, simply by adjusting the distances between the tones so that half-steps fall between 3 and 4 and between 7 and 8, and all the other distances are whole-steps.

198   It will be instructive to try a few. For instance, let us solve the problem of constructing a major scale on D. Beginning on D, take in alphabetical order the letter-names of the white notes until you have come around to D again:

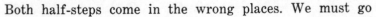

Both half-steps come in the wrong places. We must go

through the series of white notes, step by step, introducing accidentals where necessary to make the pattern fit the model of the C-major scale, with whole-steps everywhere, except between 3 and 4 and between 7 and 8. The first interval, from D to E, is all right, since it is a whole-step as it should be, but the second one must be enlarged by pushing the F up to F♯. By raising the F to F♯, we not only create a whole-step between 2 and 3, but we also simultaneously correct the distance between 3 and 4, for the F♯ now makes the desired half-step with G:

The intervals between 4 and 5, and between 5 and 6 are whole-steps as they should be, so our next problem is to widen the space between 6 and 7. This we can do in the same way by raising the C to C♯, and here again our next problem will be solved by the same stroke, for the C♯ will now make the desired half-step with the final D:

The key of D, therefore, will have two sharps in its key signature, F♯ and C♯:

199   B major will be just a little more complicated, but the same method will work. Beginning on B, take in alphabetical order the letter-names of the white notes:

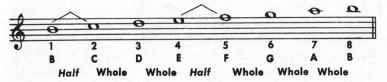

Both half-steps are in the wrong places. Between 1 and 2 we need a whole-step, so we must raise the C to C#:

But this creates a half-step (C# to D) between 2 and 3, where it is not wanted. So we now must raise the D half a step to D#:

This not only gives us the desired whole-step between 2 and 3, but at the same time puts the necessary half-step between 3 and 4, by making it D# to E, instead of D to E.

Between 4 and 5 we need another whole-step, so we must raise the F to F#:

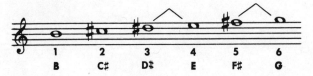

But this creates a half-step between 5 and 6 where it is not desired, so we must raise the G in turn to G♯:

1	2	3	4	5	6	7
B	C♯	D♯	E	F♯	G♯	A

Whole Whole *Half* Whole Whole *Half*

And since this, once more, creates an unwanted half-step between 6 and 7, we must raise the A to A♯:

1	2	3	4	5	6	7	8
B	C♯	D♯	E	F♯	G♯	A♯	B

Whole Whole *Half* Whole Whole Whole *Half*

This not only makes a whole-step between 6 and 7, but produces the final half-step between 7 and 8. The key of B major, then, has a key signature of five sharps, C♯ D♯ F♯ G♯ and A♯:

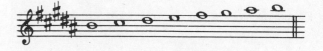

200 As an example of a scale which begins on a black key, do F♯ major. Beginning on F♯, you must take in alphabetical order the letter-names of the white notes. (The F♯ itself is a black note, of course, but the whole point of the problem is that it is given as such.)

1	2	3	4	5	6	7	8
F♯	G	A	B	C	D	E	F♯

Half *Half*

Both half-steps are in the wrong places. Between 1 and 2 we need a whole-step, so we must raise the G to G♯. But this will make a half-step between 2 and 3, so we now must raise the A to A♯:

In this way we create, at the same time, the desired half-step between 3 and 4. If you continue by the same method, you will have to raise the C to C♯, the D to D♯, and the E to E♯ (since E to F♯, wider than E to F, is a whole-step, and therefore will not do between 7 and 8).

The key of F♯ major has six sharps in its key signature, F♯ G♯ A♯ C♯ D♯ and E♯:

201   Before going any further, you should work out for yourself the major scales beginning on A, E, and C♯. You will find that A major has a key signature of three sharps, E major of four sharps, and C♯ major of seven sharps (every note is sharped in C♯ major!).

202   The major scale on F adds a slight variant of the process which is useful in other scales, too. Beginning in the usual way, take the white notes from F to F:

Although the last half-step is in the correct place, the first one is not. Let's take the intervals one at a time. Between 1 and 2, and between 2 and 3, the desired whole-steps already exist, so nothing need be done there, but between 3 and 4 the space is too *wide*, not too small as in all our previous cases. We cannot correct it by raising the A to A♯, because that would spoil the correct interval between 2 and 3, so we must *lower* the 4th degree, B, to B♭:

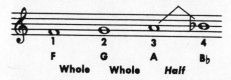

This will automatically correct the interval between 4 and 5 at the same time, since the unwanted half-step from B to C will be enlarged to B-*flat* to C, and the entire scale will now fit the pattern perfectly:

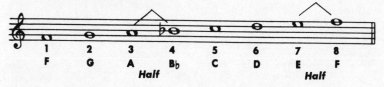

The key of F major has one flat, B♭, in its key signature:

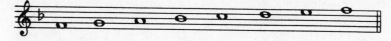

203 Try one which begins on a flatted note, Db for instance.
The series of letter-names of white notes between Db and Db
will be:

Notice that the first interval, between 1 and 2, is neither a
whole-step nor a half-step but a step-and-a-half! (D to E
would be a whole step, but this interval is widened even further by lowering its bottom member to Db; therefore it is
even half a step wider than a whole-step; i.e., a step-and-a-
half.) To correct it, we must lower the E to Eb, thereby producing the usual whole-step for the interval between 1 and
2, and at the same time automatically correcting the next
interval by changing the half-step from E to F into a whole-
step, E-*flat* to F:

But the space between 3 and 4 is still too great, so we must
reduce it to the required half-step by flatting the G:

But by doing this we have enlarged the space between 4 and
5, which was a whole-step to begin with (G to A), so that
it is now 1½ steps (Gb to A); therefore, we must proceed

as we did for the very first interval, by lowering the A to Ab:

This, of course, does the same thing to the next interval, which in turn must be reduced by lowering the B to Bb. But once this is done, the whole problem is finally solved, for the half-step between 6 and 7 becomes the correct whole-step (Bb to C) and the final half-step between 7 and 8 remains:

The key of Db major has five flats, Db Eb Gb Ab and Bb, in its key signature:

204 At this point, you must work out for yourself the major scales beginning on Bb, Eb, Ab, Gb, and Cb. You will find that their key signatures have respectively, two flats, three flats, four flats, six flats, and seven flats. (Every note is flatted in Cb major.)

205 Observe that, since C♯ and Db are really the same note on the piano keyboard, the scales of C♯ and Db will sound alike when played on the piano. The same is true for F♯ and Gb, and for Cb and B.

206 You may already have noticed that, in writing key signatures at the beginning of a piece, it is the custom not to place the sharps or flats on the staff in a haphazard manner, but to write them always in the same order. This is just a convention, but it is a useful one because the look of each signature quickly becomes familiar and the reader knows at a glance which key is intended without identifying the various accidentals or even counting them. Therefore, if you plan to continue with your music reading, it will be worth your while to memorize the following tables of key signatures. Write them several times each day, until each pattern is second nature to you:

KEY SIGNATURES, MAJOR SCALES

THE MINOR SCALE

207 All of this discussion has been concerned with the major scale, which was described as the scale most frequently used by European and American composers during the past few hundred years. Another important scale during this period has been the **minor scale,** which has its own characteristic

arrangement of half- and whole-steps. Just as the series of
white notes beginning on C serves as the model for the major
scale, so *the series of white notes beginning on A serves as
model for the minor scale:*

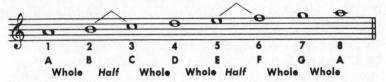

	1	2	3	4	5	6	7	8
	A	B	C	D	E	F	G	A
	Whole	Half	Whole	Whole	Half	Whole	Whole	

In minor scales, the half-steps occur between 2 and 3, and
between 5 and 6. You can construct a minor scale on any
note by observing this pattern.

208 In other words, the major scale on C uses the natural
half-steps, B to C and E to F, with no accidentals, and the
minor scale on A uses the same natural half-steps, with no
accidentals, although these half-steps fall between different
degrees of the scale in minor than in major. This means that
C major and A minor* have the same key signature — no
flats or sharps.

209 Similarly, for every major scale, there is a minor scale
that uses the same key signature, and that minor scale will
be the one beginning on the 6th degree of the major scale,
just as A is the 6th degree in the scale of C. So, if you want
to know which minor scale has the same key signature as
F major (one flat), you have only to take the 6th degree of
the F major scale, which is D, and the answer is D minor.
If you want to know which minor scale has the same key

---

*Some books use capital letters to indicate names of major scales
and small letters to indicate minor scales. This permits them to
tell the reader with a single letter, as a sort of shorthand, not
only the name of the scale but also whether it is major or minor.
For example, *A* would mean A major and *a* would mean A minor.

signature as F♯ major (six sharps), take the 6th degree
of F♯ major, which is D♯, and the answer is D♯ minor. For
G major, the 6th degree is E, so the same key signature (one
sharp) will be shared by E minor.

210 Now, in actual practice, the pattern of the minor scale is
less rigidly maintained than is that of the major. This is
because the whole-step between 7 and 8 in minor makes the
pull toward the tonic weaker than in major, where the distance to the tonic is only a half-step; consequently the 7th
degree in minor is often (but not always) raised in imitation
of the major, and the 6th degree is sometimes (but not
always) raised along with it in order to smooth over the
motion from 6 to the raised 7. Even when this is done, the
same key signature is kept for the minor scale, the extra
accidentals required for the raising of the 6th or 7th degrees
being written on the staff each time they are desired. For
example, the following melody is in A minor, with no flats
or sharps in the key signature, although there is a G♯, representing a raised 7th degree, in measure 3:

Ophelia's Song in "Hamlet"

211 The form of the minor scale outlined on page 151 is known
as the *natural minor scale*. When its 7th degree is raised
to make a half-step between 7 and 8, the resulting scale is
called the *harmonic minor scale*:

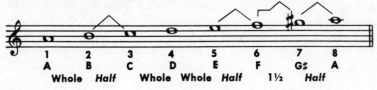

When, in addition to the raising of the 7th degree, the 6th degree is raised along with it, the new scale is called the *melodic minor scale,* and the two raised tones are used only when the melody ascends; in descending passages in melodic minor, the 6th and 7th degrees are restored to the original condition in which they occurred in the natural minor scale, since the 7th step (and the 6th with it) is no longer heading upward toward the tonic but downward away from it:

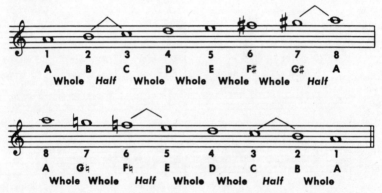

Notice that in all three cases the 3rd degree of the minor scale is only half a step from the 2nd, instead of a whole-step as in major; this is the most characteristic feature of minor scales.

212 Since you now must realize that each key signature has two possible meanings (a major scale, and the minor scale beginning on its 6th degree), you may wonder how one can judge from the key signature what the key may be. The truth of the matter is that the key signature alone is not infallible as a guide, but taken together with certain other indications, it will usually give the necessary information. For example, in "Ophelia's song" (page 152) we have a key signature of no sharps or flats, indicating either C major or A minor; but the two most prominent points in the piece, the beginning and the end, are on the note A, so we have strong reason to believe that A is the tonic, rather than C. Moreover, the G♯ in measure 3 would have no place in C major, but is frequently found in A minor as a raised 7th degree.

213 We now should revise our table of key signatures so that the two meanings of each signature are indicated:

KEY SIGNATURES, MAJOR AND MINOR SCALES

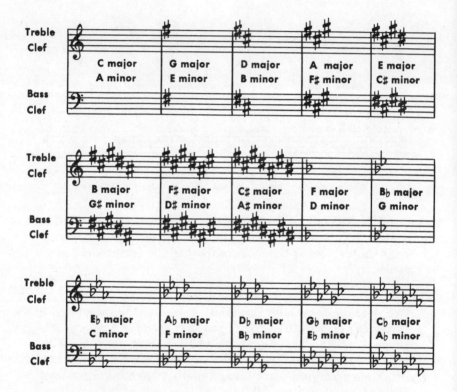

Vocabulary of Some Important

Foreign Terms Used in Music

These terms are presented here in groups, according to subject matter.

In general, the Italian terms are the most widely used. Their German and French equivalents, and an English equivalent or explanation, are given wherever applicable. Where no German or French is given, it may be assumed that no exact equivalent exists and that the Italian form is used in all languages.

214 Terms used to indicate TEMPO

	ITALIAN	FRENCH	GERMAN	ENGLISH
S	*Lento*	*Lent*	*Langsam*	Slow
L	*Largo*	*Large*	*Breit*	Broad
O	*Adagio* (literally, "At ease," but usually means "Slow," sometimes with connotation of "drawn out")			
W	*Grave*	*Lourd*	*Schwer*	Heavy, Serious
	Larghetto (diminutive of *Largo;* not so broad as *Largo*) *			

	ITALIAN	FRENCH	GERMAN	ENGLISH
M	*Andante* (literally, "going" or "walking")	*Allant*	*Gehend*	Medium slow
E	*Moderato*	*Modéré*	*Mässig*	Moderate
D	*Allegretto* (diminutive of *Allegro;* less fast than *Allegro*)			
I **U** **M**	*Andantino* (Musicians disagree on the meaning added to *Andante* by the diminutive suffix "-ino," some claiming that it means "less slow than *Andante*," others pointing out that *Andante* means "going," rather than "slow," and that *Andantino* therefore signifies "less going than *Andante*," i.e., even slower!) *			

	ITALIAN	FRENCH	GERMAN	ENGLISH
F	*Allegro* (literally, "happy")	*Animé, Vite*	*Schnell*	Fast
A	*Vivace*	*Vif*	*Lebhaft*	Lively
S	*Presto*	*Très vite*	*Sehr schnell, Eilig*	Very fast
	Vivacissimo (even livelier than *Vivace*)			
T	*Prestissimo* (even faster than *Presto*)			

-ino *-etto* In general, the diminutive suffix, -ino or -etto, added to one of the basic tempo indications, implies less of the quality of the original term, i.e., weakens it.

issimo In general, the augmentative suffix, -issimo, added to one of the basic tempo indications, implies more of the quality of the original term, i.e., intensifies it.

non troppo	*pas trop*———	*nicht zu*———	not too——— (slow, fast, etc.)

*When *Andantino, Adagietto,* or *Larghetto* is used as the *title* of a composition, the diminutive ending often refers to the proportions of the piece, rather than to its tempo; e.g., *Andantino* then signifies "an *Andante* of small proportions."

215   Terms used to indicate CHANGE of TEMPO

ITALIAN	FRENCH	GERMAN	ENGLISH
accelerando (*accel.*)	*accelérer*	*beschleunigen*	getting faster
stringendo (*string.*)	*en pressant*	*drängend*	rushing
ritardando (*rit., ritard.*)	*ralentir, ralentissant*	*zurückhalten*	slow down, retard, hold back
rallentando (*rall.*)	*ralentir, ralentissant*	*langsamer werden*	slowing down
allargando (*allarg.*)	*élargissant*	*verbreitern*	getting broader
ritenuto (*riten.*)	*retenu*	*zurückgehalten*	held back
più	*plus*	*mehr*	more

(The prefatory adverb, *più*, used with a tempo indication means "more," e.g., *più allegro* means "more *allegro*," or "faster.")

meno	*moins*	*weniger*	less

(The prefatory adverb, *meno*, used with a tempo indication means "less," e.g., *meno allegro* means "less *allegro*," or "slower.")

più mosso (more movement)	*plus mouvementé*	*bewegter*	faster
meno mosso (less movement)	*moins mouvementé*	*weniger bewegt*	slower
a tempo	*au mouvement*	*in Zeitmass*	in tempo

(used to restore the main tempo after a slowing down or speeding up)

Tempo Primo (*Tempo I°.*)	*Premier nuvement*	*Erstes Zeitmass*	First tempo

(used to restore the first tempo when some other has intervened)

L'istesso tempo	*Même mouvement*	*Dasselbe Zeitmass*	The same tempo

(used to confirm the continuance of the same tempo where the reader might imagine for some reason that it could change)

216   Terms used to indicate VOLUME of SOUND

The Italian words (and abbreviations) are ordinarily used in all languages:

forte (𝒇)	loud
piano (𝒑)	soft
fortissimo (𝒇𝒇)	very loud
pianissimo (𝒑𝒑)	very soft
mezzo forte (𝒎𝒇)	medium loud
mezzo piano (𝒎𝒑)	medium soft

Levels louder than 𝒇𝒇 are indicated by adding additional 𝒇s:

$$𝒇𝒇𝒇 \qquad 𝒇𝒇𝒇𝒇$$

Levels softer than 𝒑𝒑 are indicated by adding additional 𝒑s:

$$𝒑𝒑𝒑 \quad , \quad 𝒑𝒑𝒑𝒑 \quad .$$

217   Terms used to indicate CHANGE of VOLUME

ITALIAN	FRENCH	GERMAN	ENGLISH
crescendo (cresc.)	*en croissant*	*wachsend*	growing louder
decrescendo (decresc.) *diminuendo* (dim.)	*diminuer*	*diminuieren, vermindern*	growing softer

The Italian words, *crescendo*, *decrescendo*, and *diminuendo*, and their abbreviations, are usually used in all languages, but the French and German equivalents given above are found occasionally. Very often, instead of the word *crescendo*, the sign ⬿⬿⬿ is used to indicate "growing louder"; and instead of the words *decrescendo* or *diminuendo*, the sign ⟩⟩⟩ is used to indicate "growing softer."

fortepiano (𝒇𝒑)	*(used in all languages)*	"begin the note loud, but drop it to soft immediately"
sforzando, sforzato (𝒔𝒇 , 𝒇𝒛 , 𝒔𝒇𝒛)	*(used in all languages)*	"forced, accented"
più *meno* *non troppo*	These terms, already defined in connection with tempo, are also used in connection with volume.	

218 Terms used to indicate SIMULTANEOUS REDUCTION of TEMPO and VOLUME

ITALIAN	FRENCH	GERMAN	ENGLISH
calando (cal.)	diminuer	nachlassen	decreasing
smorzando (smorz.)	en s'effaçant	verlöschen	dying away
morendo (mor.)	en mourant	ersterben	dying down

219 Qualifying terms used to indicate MOOD, DEGREE, INTENSITY, or STYLE

ITALIAN	FRENCH	GERMAN	ENGLISH
molto	très, beaucoup	sehr, viel	very, much
poco } un poco }	un peu	ein wenig	a little
poco a poco	peu à peu	allmählich	little by little
più	plus	mehr	more
meno	moins	weniger	less
———non troppo / non troppo——— / ———ma non troppo	pas trop———	nicht zu———	not too———
agitato	agité	aufgeregt, (lebhaft) bewegt	agitated
amabile	aimable (ment)	lieblich	affectionately
animato	animé-	belebt	spirited, animated
appassionato	passioné	leidenschaftlich	passionately

Qualifying terms used to indicate MOOD, DEGREE, INTENSITY, or STYLE (Continued)

ITALIAN	FRENCH	GERMAN	ENGLISH
cantabile	chantant	gesangvoll	singing
con anima	animé, avec verve	munter	with spirit
con brio	brillant	brillant	with brilliance (dash, fire)
con dolore	avec douleur	schmerzlich	with grief
con forza	avec force	mit Kraft	with strength
con fuoco	avec ardeur, ardent	feurig	fiery, with fire
con moto	mouvementé	bewegt	with movement
dolce	doux, doucement	zart, sanft	sweetly
dolente	dolent, douloureux	klagend	grieving
energico	énergiquement	energisch	energetically
espressivo	expressif	ausdrucksvoll	expressively
giocoso	en badinant	scherzhaft	jestingly, playfully
grazioso	gracieux	graziös, zierlich	gracefully
legato	lié	gebunden	smoothly slurred
leggiero	léger	leicht	lightly
lusingando	caressant	schmeichelnd	cajolingly, alluringly
maestoso	majestueux	feierlich	majestically
marziale	martial	kriegerisch	martially
misterioso	mystérieux	geheimnisvoll	mysteriously
perdendosi	en s'effaçant	verlöschend	dying away
pesante	pesant, lourd	wichtig, schwer	heavily
piacevole	plaisant	gefällig	pleasingly, agreeably

Qualifying terms used to indicate MOOD, DEGREE, IN-
TENSITY, or STYLE (Continued)

ITALIAN	FRENCH	GERMAN	ENGLISH
portamento	port de voix	getragen	sliding of the voice (or instrument) from one tone to another
risoluto	résolu	entschlossen	resolutely
scherzando	en badinant	scherzend	playfully, jokingly
sostenuto	soutenu	getragen	sustained
staccato	(court et détaché)	(kurz abgestossen)	short and detached
teneramente	tendrement	zärtlich	tenderly
tenuto	tenu	gehalten	held

The C-Clefs

220 On pages 71 and 72 it was explained that the G-clef is used for high voices and instruments and the F-clef for low voices and instruments. That is to say, from the whole series of lines which make up the Great Staff, the top five (marked with a clef sign on the G-line) are used separately whenever there would be no use for low notes, and the bottom five (marked with a clef sign on the F-line) may be used separately when there would be no use for high notes:

For high voices
and instruments
For low voices
and instruments

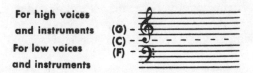

THE ALTO CLEF

221 Now, if one is dealing with voices or instruments which use chiefly the middle of the Great Staff — voices like the alto, for example, and instruments like the viola — neither of these five-line groups is perfectly suited, for such middle-of-the-road instruments would have no need for the very lowest and the very highest notes. Therefore, in writing for alto or viola, we may take the middle five lines of the Great Staff,

leaving off the top three lines of the upper staff, and the

bottom three lines of the lower staff. When these five lines are written separately there is no need to use a broken line for Middle C, the broken line having been introduced only because the original series of *eleven* lines was too much for the eye to grasp at once (see page 70). The clef which is used for these lines is a C-clef, that is, the line of Middle C is the one that is labeled with the symbolic letter. It looks like this:

222 This clef is called the **alto clef** because of its origins, although nowadays it is seldom used by alto singers, who ordinarily read in the more common treble (G) clef which the sopranos use. Its chief use today is for the viola, and even the viola sometimes reads from the treble clef when its music goes up very high.

THE TENOR CLEF

223 For tenor voices, it used to be customary to employ a slightly different form of this idea. Since the tenor sang notes a little lower than the alto's, although still in the middle region, only one line of the upper staff was retained along with three lines of the lower staff:

The C-line (Middle C again) is marked with a C-clef symbol, as in the case of the alto clef, but here it comes out on the next higher line.

224   In this position, the C clef is called the **tenor clef,** although today it is used less for the tenor voice than for the higher notes of the 'cello, bassoon, and trombone (occasionally the double-bass). For their lower notes, these instruments read in the bass (F) clef.

HYBRID CLEFS

225   As for tenor singers, the strange custom has grown up in recent years for them to pretend that they are reading in treble clef, like sopranos, but actually to produce the sounds an octave lower! Sometimes, to show that the tenor's treble clef is not a real one, it is printed as a double clef,

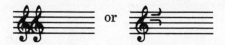

or with an *8* (to show the octave lower) attached to it,

In other words, instead of indicating Middle C for a tenor voice by the use of the tenor clef, in this way, as you might expect: , most publishers would indicate this

note an octave higher than it is intended, or perhaps with one of the hybrid double-clefs:

COMPARISON OF CLEFS

226   By way of summary, let us compare how Middle C and other tones look in each clef:

Great Staff	Treble Clef	Bass Clef	Alto Clef	Tenor Clef	"Hybrid" Tenor Clef
Middle C	Middle C	Middle C	Middle C	Middle C	Middle C
F above Middle C	F above Middle C	F above Middle C	F above Middle C	F above Middle C	F above Middle C
G below Middle C	G below Middle C	G below Middle C	G below Middle C	G below Middle C	G below Middle C

Remember that as you read across the page from left to right, you are reading exactly the same sound in each clef. All six of those Cs are Middle C, not an octave higher or lower, and all six Fs are the same F.

NAMES OF OCTAVES

227 In discussions in the theory of music, in order to distinguish one octave of a letter-name from another (a low C from a high C, for instance), the various octaves are assigned names or numbers. The following table should show you how this works:

228 The notes of the Three-lined and Four-lined Octaves involve so many leger lines that they are hard to read in their original notation. Therefore, they are sometimes written an octave lower with an **octave sign** (8va) above them to show their true meaning:

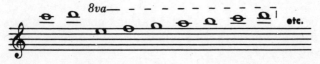

Even with the aid of this method, as you will observe, a number of leger lines cannot be avoided.

229 For the extremely low notes of the Contra Octave and Sub-contra Octave, a similar method is used to avoid some of the leger lines:

For the low octaves, this octave sign is written *below* the notes, and careful musicians usually write "8ᵛᵃ **bassa**" ("low octave") to make sure that there is no confusion with the octave sign for high notes.

230 Note that the letter-names in the Great Octave are written in capital letters, those of the Small Octave in small letters, those in the one-lined Octave with one "line" or "prime mark" after each letter, the Two-lined Octave with two lines after each, etc. In the Contra Octave, a line is used below and in front of the capital letter; and in the Sub-contra Octave, a double line is used in this position. Some writers use little index numbers instead of lines, so that instead of d″ and e′′′, you may see d^2 and e^3. Similarly they might use $_2$A for the Sub-contra Octave instead of ͵͵A.

Identification of Notes in Section 87, Page 74

1.B	2.C	3.D	4.G	5.F	6.F	7.A	8.A
9.B	10.G	11.E	12.F	13.F	14.A	15.E
16.B	17.C	18.D	19.D	20.G	21.E	22.G

Identification of Notes in Section 104*, Page 85

1. The A above Middle C
2. The Ab above Middle C
3. The G♯ above Middle C
4. The second G♯ above Middle C
5. The Eb above Middle C
6. The C♯ immediately above Middle C
7. The second A above Middle C
8. The C two octaves above Middle C
9. The B♯ above Middle C
10. The F♯ above Middle C
11. The Gb above Middle C
12. The Bb above Middle C
13. The Db above Middle C
14. The second Eb above Middle C
15. The second F♯ above Middle C
16. The A♯ above Middle C
17. The second C♯ above Middle C
18. The second D♯ above Middle C
19. The F below Middle C
20. The second A below Middle C

21. The second Bb below Middle C
22. The D below Middle C
23. The F♯ below Middle C
24. The Ab below Middle C
25. The Bb below Middle C
26. The second A♯ below Middle C
27. The C♯ below Middle C
28. The D♯ below Middle C
29. The G♯ below Middle C
30. The second Ab below Middle C
31. The second Gb below Middle C
32. The second F♯ below Middle C
33. The second Eb below Middle C
34. The Eb below Middle C
35. The second C♯ below Middle C
36. The Db below Middle C
37. The Gb below Middle C
38. The C♯ immediately above Middle C (Cf. No. 6)
39. The D above Middle C

*For formal nomenclature of notes, according to the octaves in which they appear, see Section 227, page 167

INDEX

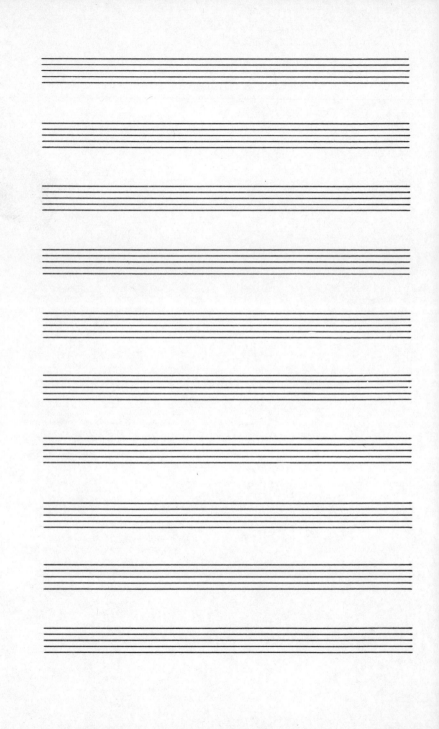

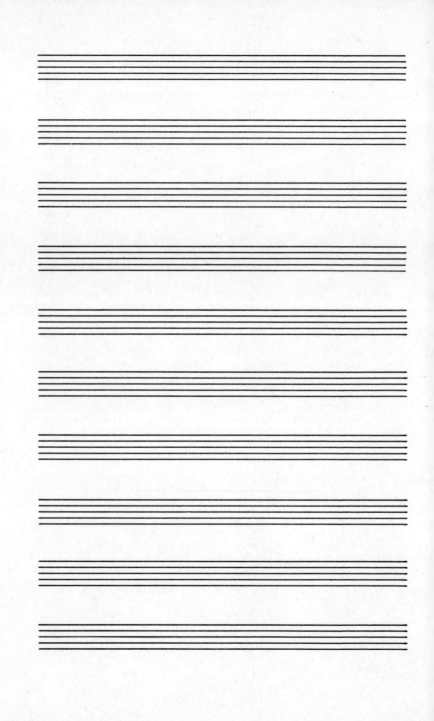

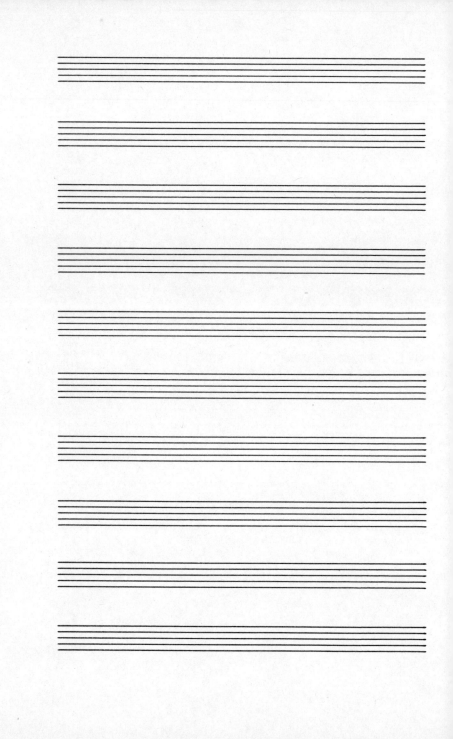